400 mind-bending IQ puzzles

Philip Carter

D&B PUBLISHING

www.dandbpublishing.com

First published in 2009 by D&B Publishing.

British Library Cataloguing-in-Publication Data
A catalogue record for this book is available from the British Library.

ISBN 978-1-904468-33-2

All sales enquiries should be directed to D&B Publishing:
Tel: 01273 711443, e-mail: info@dandbpublishing.com,
Website: www.dandbpublishing.com

Cover design by Horatio Monteverde.
Printed and bound in Finland by WSBookwell.

CONTENTS

puzzle books from D&B publishing

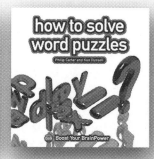

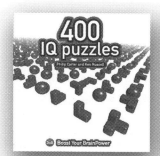

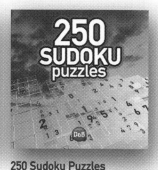

INTRODUCTION

Although it is difficult to define intelligence there is, nevertheless, at least one particularly apposite definition: *the capacity to learn and understand.*

Of all the different methods which purport to measure intelligence, the most famous is the IQ (Intelligence Quotient) test, which is a standardised test designed to measure human intelligence as distinct from attainments.

Intelligence quotient is an age-related measure of intelligence level and is described as 100 times the mental age. The word quotient means the result of dividing one quantity by another, and one definition of intelligence is mental ability or quickness of mind.

Typically, IQ tests consist of a graded series of tasks, each of which has been standardised with a large representative population of individuals in order to establish an average IQ for each test.

It is generally accepted by advocates of IQ testing that a person's mental age remains constant in development to about the age of 13, after which it is shown to slow up, and beyond the age of 18 little or no improvement is found.

When the IQ of a child is measured, the subject attempts an IQ test that has been standardised, with an average score recorded for each age group. Thus a 10-year old child who scored the result that would be expected of a 12-year old would have an IQ of 120, or 12/10 x 100.

Because after the age of 18 little or no improvement is found, adults have to be judged on an IQ test whose average score is 100, and the results graded above and below this norm according to known test scores. Like so many distributions found in nature, the distribution of IQ takes the form of a fairly regular bell curve in which similar proportions occur both above and below the norm of 100 IQ.

Although it is claimed that it is not possible, in adulthood, to increase your actual IQ, paradoxically it is possible to improve your performance on IQ tests by practising the many different types of question, and learning to recognise the recurring themes. By constant practise on different IQ tests, and by getting your mind attuned to the different types of question you may encounter, it is possible to improve your IQ rating by several percentage points.

IQ tests are set and used on the assumption that when taking the tests you know nothing about the testing method and very little about the question methods within the tests. It follows, therefore, that if you learn about this form of testing and how to approach the different types of questions, you can improve your performance on the tests themselves.

Although IQ tests measure a variety of different types of ability such as verbal, mathematical, spatial and reasoning skills, it is now becoming increasingly recognised that there are many different types of intelligence and that a high measured IQ, although desirable, is not the only key to success in life. Other characteristics such as outstanding artistic, creative or practical prowess, especially if combined with personal characteristics such as ambition, good temperament and compassion, could result in an outstanding level of success despite a low measured IQ.

Nevertheless, during the past 25-30 years IQ testing, in tandem with personality profile testing, has been brought into widespread use by employers because of the need to ensure they place the right people in the right job at the outset. One of the main reasons for this is the high cost of errors in today's world of tight budgets and reduced profit margins. To recruit a new member of staff an employer has to advertise, consider each application; reduce the applicants to a short list, interview and then train the successful applicant. If the wrong hiring choice has been made, then the whole expensive process has to be repeated.

As well as providing valuable practise on the type of questions likely to be encountered, the use of IQ tests and puzzles can be of immense value in pushing out the boundaries of our brainpower beyond what we may think possible.

Our brain needs exercise and care in the same way as other parts of the body. We eat the right foods to keep our heart healthy, we moisturize our skin to keep it from drying out and, just as gymnasts strive to increase their performance at whatever level they are competing by means of punishing training schedules and refinement of technique, there are exercises, or mental gymnastics, we can do to increase the performance of our brain and enhance quickness of thought.

Note

Because they have been newly compiled, the tests that follow in this book have not been standardised, so a precise IQ assessment cannot be provided. Nevertheless, there is a guide to performance at the end of each test, and there is also a cumulative guide for your overall performance on all ten tests.

Instructions

Each test consists of 40 questions.

A time limit of **120 minutes** is allowed for the completion of all 40 questions. You should keep strictly to this time limit; otherwise your assessment rating will be invalidated.

The use of calculators is not permitted in respect of the numerical questions, which are designed to test your aptitude when working with numbers as well as your powers of mental arithmetic.

It is recommended that you read the instructions to each question before attempting to solve it.

If you have time to spare at the end of the test use the extra time to have a quick review of your answers. You do not get any extra marks for finishing early, also we have all been guilty of slips of the pen at one time or another and this may well be one of those occasions!

Use the following tables to assess your performance.

One Test:		**Ten Tests:**	
Score	**Rating**	**Score**	**Rating**
36-40	Exceptional	350-400	Exceptional
31-35	Excellent	290-349	Excellent
25-30	Very Good	230-289	Very Good
19-24	Good	180-229	Good
14-18	Average	130-179	Average

Analysis

In addition to the above general Performance Rating, it is recommended you analyse your performance for each of the three types of questions– Verbal aptitude, Numerical aptitude and Spatial aptitude.

An analysis of individual scores for each of these three types of questions will enable you to build and capitalise on your strengths, and work on improving performance in areas of weakness.

Verbal Aptitude

Verbal intelligence is a measurement of your capacity to use language in order to express yourself, comprehend written text and understand other people.

People who possess a high level of verbal skills often excel in fields such as writing (author, journalist, editing, critic), teaching (language, drama), legal profession (judge/barrister/lawyer), personnel work (advocate, human resources, counsellor) and as actors, psychologists, interpreters and interviewers.

Numerical Aptitude

Mathematical intelligence tests generally explore your ability to reason and to perform basic arithmetic functions.

Good mathematical ability is an excellent stepping stone to career success in jobs such as accounting or banking.

People who possess a high level of numerical skills also often excel in jobs such as; auditor, business consultant, financial analyst, mathematics or science teacher, quantity surveyor, tax adviser, company secretary, computer programmer or stockbroker.

Spatial Aptitude

The ability being investigated in questions of spatial aptitude is how well a person is able to identify patterns and meaning from what might appear at first glance random or very complex information.

This type of abstract reasoning does not involve problems that are verbal or numerical in nature.

As Spatial aptitude involves quite different thought processes to those which determine verbal or numerical aptitude, it is quite common for people who score very highly on numerical and verbal aptitude tests to score equally badly on spatial aptitude tests and vice versa.

This is because the left side of the human brain is analytical and functions in a sequential and logical fashion and is the side which controls language, academic studies and rationality. The right side of the brain is creative and intuitive and leads, for example, to the birth of ideas for works of art and music and is the side of the brain which determines how well we are able to adapt to tests of spatial aptitude. As many people have some degree of brain bias, they thus perform better on tests which involve thought processes controlled by the stronger side of their brain.

People who scored badly on the tests in this section, after performing well on the verbal and numerical aptitude tests, should, therefore, have no great cause for concern. They have, however, the opportunity to practise and increase their performance on this type of spatial aptitude testing and to develop their right-brain thinking.

People who possess a high level of spatial aptitude often excel in fields such as architecture, photography, engineering design, decorating, and as artists, carpenters, landscape designers, cartoon animators, guides, fashion designers, and civil engineers.

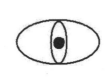

Draw the missing ellipse in the above sequence.

7	9	12	16
11	13		20
14		19	23
16	18		25

Which is the missing section?

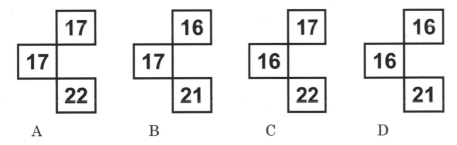

     A   B   C   D

Alf is 1 ½ times as old as Sid, and Sid is 1 ½ times as old as Jim.
How old are Alf, Sid and Jim if their combined ages total 171?

Find two 8-letter words that are antonyms by moving clockwise from circle to circle. You must find the starting point for each word. Each word starts in a different circle and the letters in each word appear in consecutive circles.

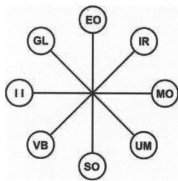

A   C   ?   H   ?   M   P   R   U   W   Z

Which two letters should replace the question marks?

Place a word in the brackets that means the same as the definitions either side of the brackets.

machination   (   )   area of land

The ***** in the *****   ***** very old and *****, as ***** they had ***** their ***** too *****, and ***** new *****.

Insert the following ten words into the sentence in the correct position in order for it to make sense.

though	needed	skins	elephants	looked
long	ones	zoo	worn	dusty

What is an arbalest?

a. a man-made water channel
b. an expert in the cultivation of trees
c. a dealer in foreign currencies
d. a moulding around a door or window
e. a medieval crossbow

is to

as

is to

A	B	C	D	E

What number is missing?

?	*	342
*		*
5736942		2435
*		*
246375	*	53642

Which two words are most opposite in meaning?

humane, crude, humble, genteel, awkward, pious

CLEANLY AUDITED is an anagram of which two words that are similar in meaning?

Clue: in point of fact

1 ½, 3 ¼, ? , 6 ¾, 8 ½, 10 ¼

What number should replace the question mark?

Which of the following is not an anagram of a type of bird?

heat pans

a tidal man

one pig

a pencil

cordon

Find the starting point and work from letter to adjacent letter horizontally and vertically, but not diagonally, to spell out a 12-letter word. You must provide the missing letters

Identify two words (one from each set of brackets) that form a connection (analogy), thereby relating to the words in capitals in the same way.

swerve (veer, change, direction)
rotate (deviate, gyrate, fluctuate)

Faith, Hope and Charity have £72.00 between them. Together Faith and Charity have double the amount of money that Hope has, while Hope and Charity together have the same amount of money as Faith. How much money does each have?

What familiar phrase is represented below?

O -----T ----- N

----- O ------

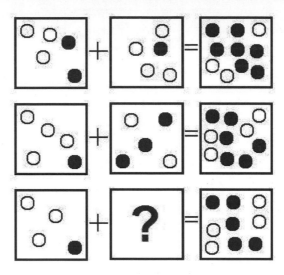

Which is the missing square?

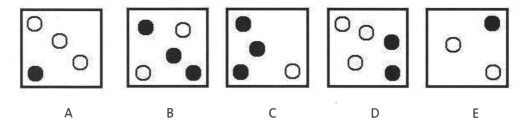

A   B   C   D   E

32 (4198) 96

65 (7388) 83

79 (?) 36

What number should replace the question mark?

Find two words, one in each circle, that are synonyms. You must find the starting point of each word and provide the missing letters. One word appears reading clockwise around one circle and the other appears reading anti-clockwise around the other circle.

The ages of a group of people are:

47, 36, 29, 15, 64, 35, 82, 12, 28, 52

What percentage of people in the group are below the average age for the group?

Only one group of 5 letters below can be re-arranged to spell out a 5-letter word in the English language. Identify the word.

WIZOL   GOBEH

UCLDI   NEULH

DIMUS   OABTL

Which word is the odd one out?

cerebrum, aorta, cortex, thalamus, cerebellum

How many different four-letter words in the English language can be produced from the four letters OPST? Each letter must be used just once in each word.

Find the feature that will determine which one of the following words is the odd one out?

moustache, pagoda, frangipane, voluntary, therapeutic

Z Y W V T S Q P ? ? ? ?

What are the next four letters in this sequence?

48		29		?	
84	22	63	33	98	31

What number should replace the question mark?

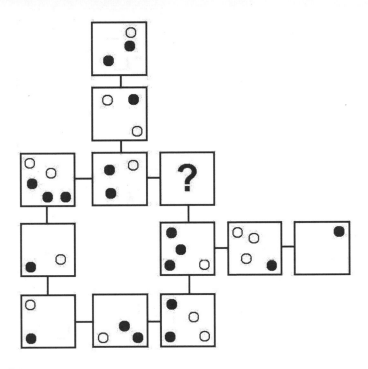

Which is the missing tile?

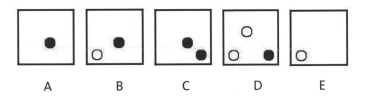

| A | B | C | D | E |

Change one letter only in each of the words below to produce a familiar phrase.

FIVE X LOG US

In order to face up to a problem head on I am seizing the bony outgrowths of a male ungulate of the species Bovidae. What am I doing?

horticulture is to gardens as agriculture is to:

fields, ground, sheep, plants, grow

Tom, Dick and Harry share out a certain sum of money between them. Tom receives 2/5, Dick receives 0.45 and Harry receives £63.00.

How much is the original amount of money?

What word can be placed in the brackets so that it forms another word or phrase when tacked onto the end of the first word, and another word or phrase when placed in front of the second word?

OVER (   ) COAT

Which word in brackets is most opposite in meaning to the word in capitals?

SECULAR (profane, sacred, united, unsafe, exposed)

An electrical circuit wiring two sets of lights depends on a system of switches A, B, C and D. Each switch when working has the following effect on a set of lights:

Switch A turns lights 1 and 2 on/off or off/on

Switch B turns lights 2 and 4 on/off or off/on

Switch C turns lights 1 and 3 on/off or off/on

Switch D turns lights 3 and 4 on/off or off/on

 ON

 OFF

In the following, switches D, C, A, B are thrown in turn, with the result that Fig 1 is transformed into Fig 2. One of the switches is not, therefore, working and has had no effect on the numbered lights.

Identify which one of the switches is not working.

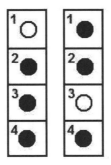

Fig. 1   Fig. 2

23	23	X	23	X
X	X	42	X	X
33	X	32	X	X
X	33	X	33	X
X	X	32	X	?

What number should replace the question mark?

What number should replace the question mark?

5	6	3
9	8	7
4	4	2
5	8	?

The clue *incorrect clanger* leads to what pair of rhyming words?

If F F the B represents the familiar phrase: Fortune Favours the Brave, what familiar phrase is represented by:

E P T a S

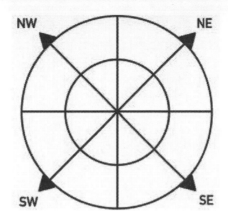

Insert the letters into the correct segments in each quadrant to produce two connected eight letter words, one reading clockwise around the outer circle and the other reading anti-clockwise around the inner circle.

NW: TIRE
NE: LAID
SE: MITU
SW: VYHE

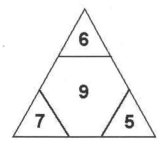 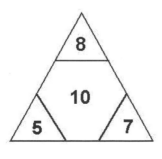 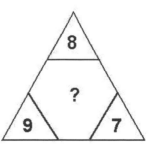

What number should replace the question mark?

Change one letter only in each of the words below to produce a familiar phrase.

AT CAR IS OWE RAN WELL

Place a word in the brackets that has the same meaning as the definitions either side of the brackets.

cut a hole (   ) train

5	2	3	6
4	5	8	7
3	9	8	2
4	6	3	?

What number should replace the question mark?

spa, pare, are, - - -

Which three letter word below completes the above list?

a. can

b. red

c. bed

d. has

e. rod

3	4	5	6
7			13
11	14		20
15	19	23	27

Which is the missing section?

A B C D

tape, head, pass, were, worm, room, word, ?

What comes next?

 calf, seal, slug, wolf or lion?

The family next door has both boy and girl children. Each of the girls has the same number of sisters as she has brothers, and each of the boys has twice as many sisters as has he has brothers.

How many boys and girls are there?

Only one group of 5 letters below can be re-arranged to spell out a 5-letter word in the English language. Identify the word.

LARTO   GLPOI   TADIM

HAONW   BAIMC   UNROP

16, 33, 67, 135, 271, ?

What number should replace the question mark?

What word in brackets is most opposite in meaning to the word in capitals?

SHIFTY (guileless, stable, meticulous, diffident, emaciated)

What number comes next?

78436, 59052, 45260, ?

Using the letters of WORDPLAY no more than twice each, what 9-letter word in the English language can be produced?

The fourth digit is three less than the second digit, the second digit is two less than the first digit and the fifth digit is one less than the second digit.

68457   64613   79467

      64273   98576

75924   53607

Which two numbers are being described?

What is the meaning of LIONISE?

a. to treat like a celebrity
b. convert assets into cash
c. eat excessively
d. bend metal on an anvil
e. toughen or strengthen

The two phrases below are each anagrams of phrases that are spelled differently, have different meanings, but sound exactly alike (as, for example, *no notion* and *known ocean*)

fondle shark   foul dancers

Which is the odd one out?

wide, expansive, broad, towering, extensive

Which set of letters is the odd set out?

JKMLN   UVXWY   DEGFH

QRTSU   GIHJK   NOQPR

The average of three numbers is 16. The average of two of these numbers is 11. What is the third number?

What is the longest word that can be produced from the following ten letters?

MUERVHANYL

Identify two words (one from each set of brackets) that form a connection (analogy), thereby relating to the words in capitals in the same way.

ABET (invoke, connive, speculate)
FACILITATE (expedite, intercede, change)

What number should replace the question mark?

98	42	5	37	16
53	6	97	14	82
48	15	96	27	?

26

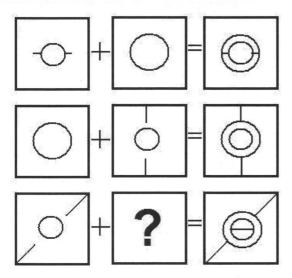

Which is the missing square?

A   B   C   D   E

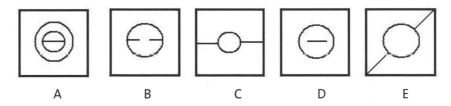

	5972836	is to	9753268
and	6917384	is to	9731468
therefore	7134826	is to	?

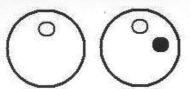

Draw the missing circle in the above sequence.

Solve the anagram in brackets to correctly complete the quotation by Ludwig Erhard

A (mice or mops) is the art of dividing a cake in such a way that everyone believes he has the biggest piece.

3	2	9	7
2	1	6	2
7	7		
1	4		

7	5	8	6
3	1	4	2
5	2		
5	0		

?	4	6	8
6	1	2	?
8	4		
4	?		

What numbers should replace the question marks?

Each square contains the letters of a 9-letter word. Find the two words that are antonyms.

D	E	E		
N	E	R		
R	T	T	V	C
		N	E	I
		N	I	E

How tall is a sapling that is 5 metres shorter than a fence that is 6 times higher than the sapling?

Which is the odd one out?

A 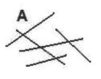 B   C

D 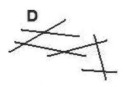 E

tolerant = epoch
knowingly = triumph
energetic = acquire

Following the rules above, what does captivate equal?

befitting, different, portfolio, atonement or colleague?

TENUOUS FORMAT is an anagram of which familiar phrase (3, 3, 2, 5 letters long)?

Clue: peter out

What word can be placed in the brackets so that it forms another word or phrase when tacked onto the end of the first word, and another word or phrase when placed in front of the second word?

sun   (   )   pot

10	5	19	7	9
21	12	3	24	4
36	15	18	14	11
1	6	44	8	2
23	17	29	30	27

Looking at straight lines of numbers either horizontally, vertically or diagonally, what number is three places away from itself plus 3, two places away from itself plus 2, two places away from itself multiplied by 2 and three places away from itself divided by 3?

Which two words are closest in meaning?

curtail, scratch, abrade, cancel, consume, destroy

What number should replace the question mark?

```
        2                               7
        6                               4
 9           3                   8           14
                  7
                  ?
           9           3
```

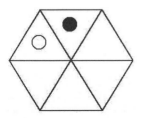 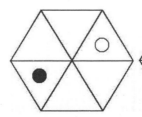 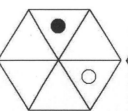 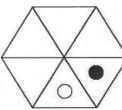

Draw the missing hexagon in the above sequence.

What number should replace the question mark?

```
  *        21      *        *
  *         *     32        *
 13         *      *       43
  *         ?      *        *
```

An electrical circuit wiring two sets of lights depends on a system of switches A, B, C and D. Each switch when working has the following effect on a set of lights:

Switch A turns lights 1 and 2 on/off or off/on

Switch B turns lights 2 and 4 on/off or off/on

Switch C turns lights 1 and 3 on/off or off/on

Switch D turns lights 3 and 4 on/off or off/on

 ON

 OFF

In the following, switches B, A, C, D are thrown in turn, with the result that Fig 1 is transformed into Fig 2. One of the switches is not, therefore, working and has had no effect on the numbered lights. Identify which one of the switches is not working.

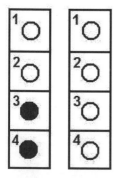

Fig. 1   Fig. 2

dry   lit   burn   flower

Which word below shares a common feature with all the four words above?

care, set, part, oak or mast?

100, 1000, 165, 935, 230, 870, 295, ?, ?

What two numbers continue the above sequence?

pastry, artful, rumble, Ulster, ?

What word continues the sequence?

homage, levity, stigma, sentry or laptop?

Alter one letter only from each word below to produce a familiar phrase.

DIVE I NOW LEAVE ON LINE

A   B   C   D   E   F   G   H

What letter is two to the right of the letter which is three to the left of the letter which is five places to the right of the letter immediately to the left of the letter D ?

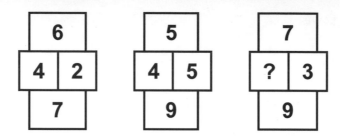

What number should replace the question mark?

Identify two words (one from each set of brackets) that form a connection (analogy), thereby relating to the words in capitals in the same way.

corolla (petals, flower, stamen)
pedicle (bud, nectary, stalk)

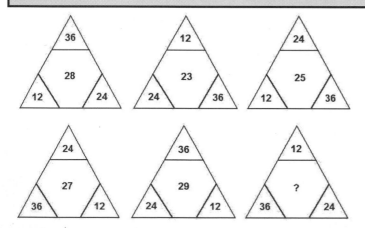

What number should replace the question mark?

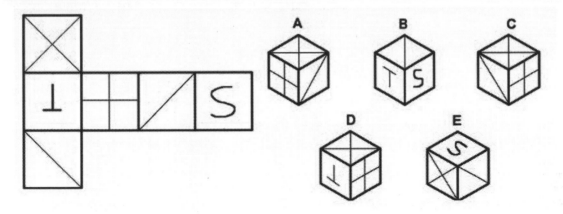

When the above is folded to form a cube, which is the only complete cube that **cannot** be produced?

What is the meaning of DIACONAL?

a. through the course of time
b. accent mark placed over a vowel
c. relating to a deacon

d. scientology
e. division into two parts

Combine three of the ten bits below to produce a word meaning: SQUEEZE.

and, int, ict, ter, con, ici, per, str, was, ler

481, 216, 202, 428, 323, ?

What three digit number comes next?

Which is the odd one out?

succinct, pithy, prolix, concise, terse

Only one group of 5 letters below can be re-arranged to spell out a 5-letter word in the English language. Identify the word.

AKDED   CUIPM   ALGEH

UFBOP   ONGYU   ECIDP

7	4	3	2	5
6	8	5	3	8
4	5	7	2	9
6	3	5	7	8

6	5	2	3	4
?	9	4	2	?
5	4	6	3	8
7	?	4	?	9

What numbers should replace the question marks?

TEAPOT HINGES is an anagram of what familiar phrase (3, 4, 5 letters long)

Clue: work out well

Which word in brackets is most opposite in meaning to the word in capitals?

PREDICTABLE (worried, vague, unlikely, strange, impartial)

Which is the missing section?

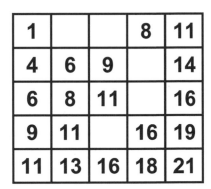

1			8	11
4	6	9		14
6	8	11		16
9	11		16	19
11	13	16	18	21

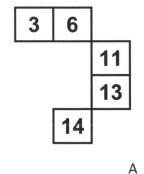 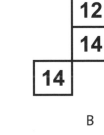 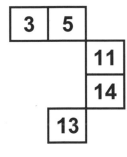 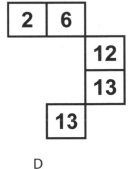

       A   B   C   D

Place a word in the brackets that has the same meaning as the definitions either side of the brackets.

an association or union   (   )   an obsolete unit of distance

What number should replace the question mark?

$$6 \qquad\qquad 9$$

$$210 \qquad\qquad 156$$

$$8 \qquad 15 \qquad 4 \qquad 12$$

$$?$$

$$132$$

$$7 \qquad 6$$

Solve the anagram in brackets to correctly complete the quotation by George Bernard Shaw.

A (Vermont Gen) that robs Peter to pay Paul can always depend on the support of Paul.

Insert a sporting term on the bottom line to complete the nine 3-letter words reading downwards.

R	F	S	T	C	H	P	P	G
A	A	E	A	O	A	A	E	E
*	*	*	*	*	*	*	*	*

Identify two words (one from each set of brackets) that form a connection (analogy), thereby relating to the words in capitals in the same way.

CONTINUAL (connected, repeated, numerous)
CONTINUOUS (frequent, unbroken, occasionally)

Which is the missing square?

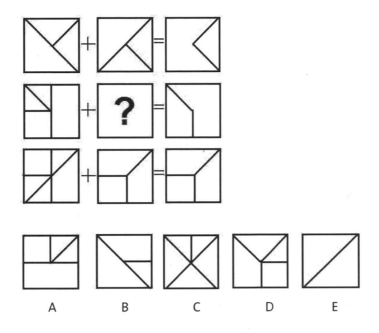

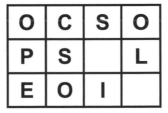

Find the starting point in order to spell out a 12-letter word by moving from letter to adjacent letter horizontally and vertically, but not diagonally. You must provide the missing letters.

2	5	7	12	19
4	6	10	16	26
6	11	17	28	45
10	17	27		
16	28	44		

Which is the missing section?

46	71
72	118

A

44	72
74	116

B

44	71
72	116

C

46	71
74	118

D

Place a word in the brackets that has the same meaning as the definitions either side of the brackets.

desist (   ) melody

CLATTERY JIM is an anagram of which two words (7, 4 letters long) that are opposite in meaning?

Clue: keep a cool head under pressure?

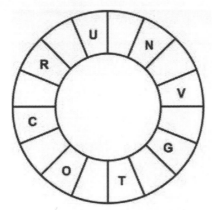

Find the starting point to spell out a 16-letter word reading clockwise. You must fill in the missing letters.

Which is the odd one out?

```
3248          9546
        7355
2146          8486
        7213
```

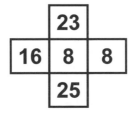
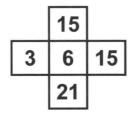
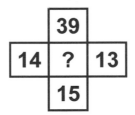

What number should replace the question mark?

Which Charles Dickens' novel creates the lousy chiropodist?

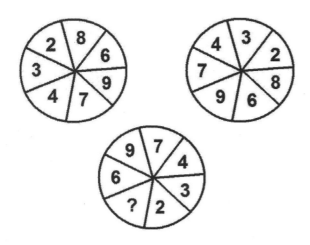

What number should replace the question mark?

If F F the B represents the familiar phrase: Fortune Favours the Brave, what familiar phrase is represented by: E P T a S ?

What word can be placed in the brackets so that it forms another word or phrase when tacked onto the end of the first word, and another word or phrase when placed in front of the second word?

head   (   )   pipe

SUNDAY
MONDAY
TUESDAY
WEDNESDAY
THURSDAY
FRIDAY
SATURDAY

i.
Eliminate the day before and the day after the day that comes two days after Monday

ii.
Eliminate the day that comes two days before the day that immediately follows Tuesday

iii.
Eliminate all the days that come either immediately before or immediately after the days you have already eliminated.

What day are you left with?

6	8
1	3

9	6
3	4

8	2
7	9

7	?
5	8

What number should replace the question mark?

Which two words are closest in meaning?

zephyr, acme, wind, rustic, fervency, oscillation

	719 358	is to	183 597
and	382 964	is to	849 623
therefore	652 734	is to	??? ???

Which is the odd one out?

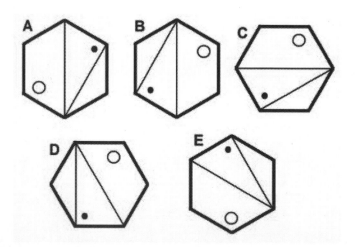

Complete the 6-letter words so that the two letters that start the second word are the same two letters that end the first word, and the two letters that start the third word are the same two letters that end the second word etc. The two letters that end the sixth word are the same two letters that start the first word, to complete the circle.

IE   **CO**

ND   **DD**

IG   **NG**

3	9	5	6
1	7	9	2
4	6	7	8
2	8	3	?

What number should replace the question mark?

Place a word in the brackets that has the same meaning as the definitions either side of the brackets.

assuage(   )   anneal

What is the value of: ¾ ÷ ½ ?

Which two words are closest in meaning?

concierge, portable, foreboding, compact, ordinary, modern

What number should replace the question mark?

72	73	83	43
24	52	?	36
28	27	17	57
76	48	71	64

The phrase below has had its initial letters and word boundaries removed. What is the phrase?

HEEAROT

Seven bags of sugar have weights in kilograms of consecutive odd numbers, with their weights averaging 7 kilograms.

What is the weight of the heaviest bag of sugar?

A familiar phrase has had its initial letters and word boundaries removed. What is the phrase? All remaining letters are in the correct order.

SHEASEAYE

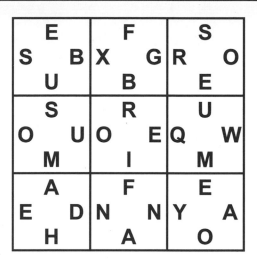
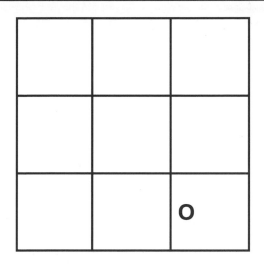

Rearrange the 9 squares in the second grid so that each adjacent pair of letters on the inside spells out a 2-letter word (12 words in total), and two related words appear reading clockwise around the outer perimeter.

A book has 98 pages plus two thirds of its total number of pages. How many pages has the book?

Identify two words (one from each set of brackets) that form a connection (analogy), thereby relating to the words in capitals in the same way.

WHY (how, soon, because)

WHICH (that, when, who)

The time is 17 minutes to the hour on a clock in which the numbers on the face are shown in Roman numerals. Arrange the numerals below in the order in which they appear from the minute hand reading anti-clockwise.

XII   V   III   IX   VII

OVERHEAT AN HEN is an anagram of which phrase (6, 2, 5 letters long)?

Clue: Utopia

A	D
B	C

C	I
E	G

E	N
H	K

?	?
?	?

What letters should appear in the final square?

If five men can build a house in 27 days, how long will it take twelve men to build the same house if they all work at the same rate?

Identify two words (one from each set of brackets) that form a connection (analogy), thereby relating to the words in capitals in the same way.

MALE (buck, cob, jack)   FEMALE (sow, pen, mare)

What number should replace the question mark?

	9				12	
4	56	7	3	72	12
	5			6	

	7	
6	**?**	4
	5	

is to

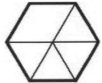

as

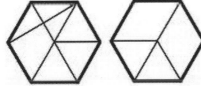

is to

A	B	C	D

Sunday, Monday, Wednesday, Saturday, Wednesday, Monday, ?

Which day comes next?

cannon is to fire as rocket is to: projectile, launch, aim, war, space

Place a word in the brackets that means the same as the definitions outside the brackets.

Spick and span   (   )   type of tree

Solve the anagram in brackets to correctly complete the quotation by Mark Twain.

Few things are harder to put up with than the (CAN ANYONE) of a good example.

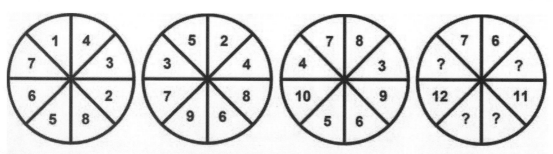

What numbers should replace the question marks?

What word in brackets is most opposite in meaning to the word in capitals?

CURRENT (maladroit, worn, archaic, wrinkled, contemporary)

Which is the odd one out?

dramatize, disparage, deprecate, diminish, decry

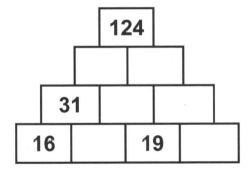

Each block is equal in value to the sum of the two numbers immediately below it. Fill in all the missing numbers.

What word can be placed in the brackets so that it forms another word or phrase when tacked onto the end of the first word, and another word or phrase when placed in front of the second word?

boot   (   )   fire

How many minutes is it before 12 noon if 35 minutes ago it was four times as many minutes past 10 a.m.?

SPIES RAID LABS is an anagram of which two words that are similar in meaning?

Clue: Shangri-La

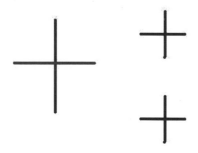

How can you add four lines to the above arrangement to produce five?

```
*    *    *    *    *    *    *
L    O    W    V    O    C    R
S    O    I    A    V    O    I
*    *    *    *    *    *    *
```

Insert two countries, one on the top line and one on the bottom line to produce seven four-letter words reading downwards.

An electrical circuit wiring two sets of lights depends on a system of switches A, B, C and D. Each switch when working has the following effect on a set of lights:

Switch A turns lights 1 and 2 on/off or off/on

Switch B turns lights 2 and 4 on/off or off/on

Switch C turns lights 1 and 3 on/off or off/on

Switch D turns lights 3 and 4 on/off or off/on

 ON

 OFF

In the following, switches B, C, A, D are thrown in turn, with the result that Fig 1 is transformed into Fig 2. One of the switches is not, therefore, working and has had no effect on the numbered lights.

Identify which one of the switches is not working.

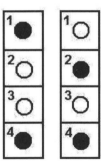

Fig. 1   Fig. 2

What is the meaning of COLLOQUY?

a. inscription   c. to arrange or place   e. to work jointly
b. row of columns   d. dialogue

S   S   T   T   A   O   ?   P   T

What letter is missing?

Which is the odd one out?

lens, Perspex, Pyrex, lunette, pipette

Only one group of 5 letters below can be re-arranged to spell out a 5-letter word in the English language. Identify the word.

AFGNE   OAKCT   AOLWF

EINTL   LURTI   ACOPD

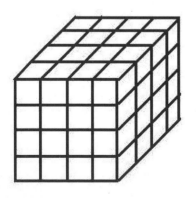

64 square blocks are glued together to form a cube. The cube is then painted red on all 6 sides. If the 64 blocks are then disassembled, how many blocks will have no paint on them?

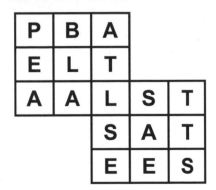

Each square contains the letters of a 9-letter word. Find the two words that are antonyms.

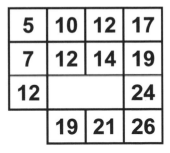

Which is the missing section?

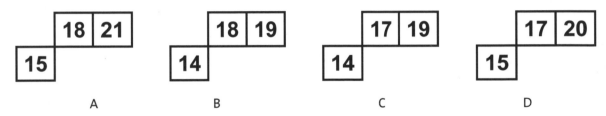

A   B   C   D

Insert the name of a river onto the bottom row to complete nine 3-letter words reading downwards.

F	L	T	B	F	T	S	M	B
I	E	O	I	U	E	I	A	E
*	*	*	*	*	*	*	*	*

Identify two words (one from each set of brackets) that form a connection (analogy), thereby relating to the words in capitals in the same way.

CANDLE (flame, wick, light)
BULB (switch, electric, filament)

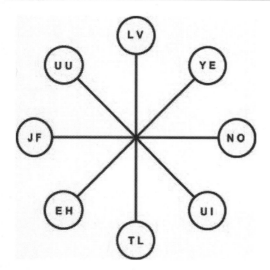

Find two 8-letter words reading clockwise that are synonyms. Each word starts in a different circle and the letters in each word are consecutive.

What word can be placed in the brackets so that it forms another word or phrase when tacked onto the end of the first word, and another word or phrase when placed in front of the second word?

over   (   )   riot

In 13 years time the combined age of my four cousins will be 83. What will it be in 9 years time?

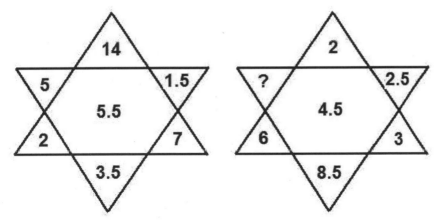

What number should replace the question mark?

What is rodomontade?

a. nonsensical speech   d. boasting
b. an Italian dish of rice and cheese   e. a gambling game
c. a form of measles

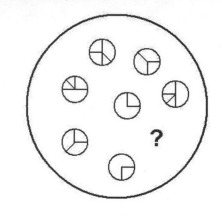

Which is the missing circle?

A   B   C   D   E

T	1S 1W	1S 1W
1E 1S	1E 1S	1N 1W
1N 2E	2N 1E	2W 2N

You must find the starting point and, by following the directional instructions, visit every square once each only, eventually arriving at the square marked with a T for treasure.

IS
1W
means move one square south and one square west.

Change one letter only in each of the words below to produce a familiar phrase.

FROG TIDE DO MIME

Only one group of 5 letters below can be re-arranged to spell out a 5-letter word in the English language. Identify the word.

CFIEL   DIUNF

                         OANJB

KAOWN   UPHRE

Ben is one and a quarter times as old as Bill. How old are Bill and Ben if their combined ages total 63?

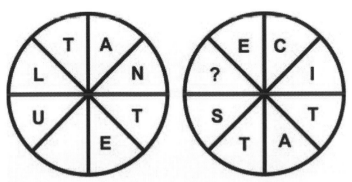

Find two 8-letter words that are synonyms. One word appears reading clockwise round one circle and the other appears anti-clockwise round the other circle.

You have to provide the missing letters

What number should replace the question mark?

48   72   56   54

       12   17

9   12   6   7

       39   40

              ?

       5   13

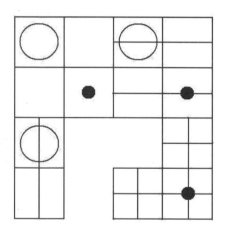
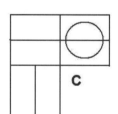
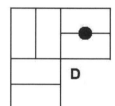

Which is the missing piece?

In order to set an example I am putting into actuality the modus operandi that I evangelise. What am I doing?

559	225	?

873	?	48

263	?	18

What numbers should replace the question marks?

callipers is to diameter as steelyard is to: density, weight, length, distance, strength

Place a word in the brackets that has the same meaning as the definitions either side of the brackets.

omnibus   (   )   instructor

Which two words are most opposite in meaning?

singular, philanthropic, penurious, apathetic, logical, graphic

Starting from North, list the following compass points in the correct order working anti-clockwise.

ESE   SW   NNE   WNW   SSW   NE   SSE

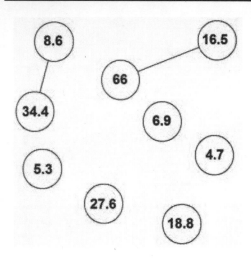

Which two pairs of unconnected numbers should be connected, and which is then the odd one out?

1	2	3	5
4		5	6
5	3		11
9	4	13	17

Which is the missing section?

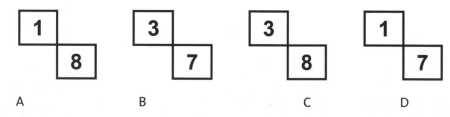

A   B   C   D

62

PLACEBO
SECLUDE
SPECIFY

What comes next?

eunuchs, eighths, hurrahs, seraphs or fourths ?

Which of the following letters can be removed from a word meaning THERAPEUTIC to produce a word meaning CENTRAL?

i. E
ii. C
iii. N
iv. T
v. L

Identify two words (one from each set of brackets) that form a connection (analogy), thereby relating to the words in capitals in the same way.

INVENTORY (list, goods, stock)
MANIFEST (ship, cargo, merchandise)

Solve the anagram in brackets to correctly complete the quotation by Philip Johnson.

(THEIR CUTE CAR) is the art of how to waste space.

Test Five: Question 28

1	2	4	8
3	6	12	24
5	14	32	68
7	26	72	?

What number should replace the question mark?

Test Five: Question 29

HATE SKY LABS is an anagram of which two words that are opposite in meaning?

Clue: steady as a rocker

Test Five: Question 30

15, 11.5, 8, 4.5, 1, ?

What number should replace the question mark to continue the sequence?

Test Five: Question 31

Which two words that are similar in meaning have been fused together? All letters appear in the correct order.

MOFINSECTARALY

An electrical circuit wiring two sets of lights depends on a system of switches A, B, C and D. Each switch when working has the following effect on a set of lights:

Switch A turns lights 1 and 2 on/off or off/on

Switch B turns lights 2 and 4 on/off or off/on

Switch C turns lights 1 and 3 on/off or off/on

Switch D turns lights 3 and 4 on/off or off/on

 ON

 OFF

In the following, switches C, A, D, B are thrown in turn, with the result that Fig 1 is transformed into Fig 2. One of the switches is not, therefore, working and has had no effect on the numbered lights.

Identify which one of the switches is not working.

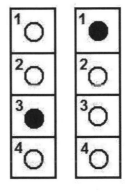

Fig. 1   Fig. 2

If F F the B represents the familiar phrase: Fortune Favours the Brave, what familiar phrase is represented by: A S L than W ?

1	3	5	7
19	16	13	10
23	27	31	35
?	?	?	?

What numbers should replace the question marks?

C	E	O	N
E	F	R	
I		S	I

Find the starting point in order to spell out a 12-letter word by moving from letter to adjacent letter horizontally and vertically, but not diagonally. You must provide the missing letters.

A   E   ?   J   N   Q   S   W   Z

What letter should replace the question mark in the above sequence?

9	0
2	6

7	3
4	5

5	6
?	?

3	9
8	3

What numbers should replace the question marks?

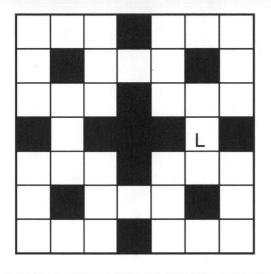

Place the twenty 3-letter words into the crossword with the aid of the letter already provided.

AIR	OAR	WET	TAR	WHO
TOR	AND	ALE	LOT	TIE
INN	ICE	APT	ROD	EAR
IMP	PIE	LIP	DID	ALL

Identify two words (one from each set of brackets) that form a connection (analogy), thereby relating to the words in capitals in the same way.

OBELISK (dagger, bullet, paragraph)
ASTERISK (punctuate, insert, star)

What is the missing number?

38	1610	72
45	455	19
57	?	23

What number should replace the question mark?

```
4    3    6    2
1    7    4    5
3    6    7    3
2    8    6    ?
```

I am laying in position the total extent of oval reproductive bodies that I possess inside a single woven container with handles. What am I doing?

KPR : MMU

MDJ : OAM

RID : ? ? ?

What day and date comes 38 days after Wednesday 12 April?

If 9 L of a C is Nine Lives of a Cat, what is represented by the following?

9 P in the S.S.

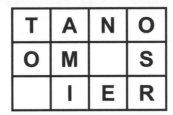

T	A	N	O
O	M		S
	I	E	R

Find the starting point in order to spell out a 12-letter word by moving from letter to adjacent letter horizontally and vertically, but not diagonally. You must provide the missing letters.

Matthew is three times as old as Amy. Five years ago he was four times as old as Amy. In how many years will he be twice as old as Amy?

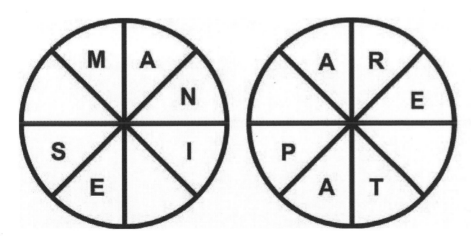

Find two 8 letter words, one in each circle that are synonyms, both reading clockwise.

Which four numbers are missing from the grid?

3	6	4	7	9	3	6
9	7	4	6	3	9	7
6	4	?	9	3	6	4
3	9	?	4	6	3	9
4	7	?	3	6	4	7
6	3	?	7	4	6	3
7	9	3	6	4	7	9

What word is suggested by the group of words below?

Pascal, Coulomb, Kelvin

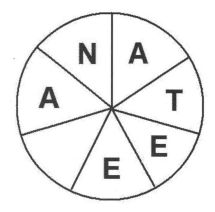

Find a seven letter word reading clockwise. You must provide the missing letter.

What phrase is represented below?

AC - -
DEG - - -
MIC - - -
KILO - - - -
CENTI - - - - -
MI - -
VO - -
AMP - - -

What word is missing from the brackets?

trims   (Christmas)   cash

lone   (   )   whale

Identify two words (one from each set of brackets) that form a connection (analogy), thereby relating to the words in capitals in the same way.

hands (gesticulate, rotate, alternate)
pendulum (swing, movement, frequency)

What word can be placed in the brackets so that it forms another word or phrase when tacked onto the end of the first word, and another word or phrase when placed in front of the second word?

acid   (   )   tube

What comes next?

A B C E F G J K L ? ? ? W X Y

What three letters are missing from the above sequence?

What is ½ of 12.5% of 1/3 of 6/9 of 72?

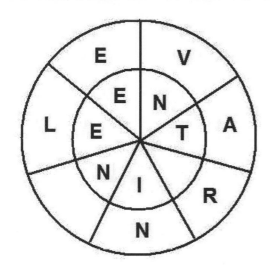

Find two 7-letter words that are antonyms, one reading clockwise around the inner circle and the other anti-clockwise around the outer circle. You must provide the missing letters.

What number should replace the question mark?

7	4	3	4
3	5	9	1
6	1	2	9
2	8	4	?

What four-letter word goes behind test, inner and torpedo?

The clue *correct eight bits* leads to what pair of rhyming words?

	FEN is to POX
and	DEED is to NOON
therefore	CUBED is to ?

DID TRUCE is an anagram of two this and that words, CUT, DRIED (cut and dried).

BLEAK WITCH is an anagram of which two other this and that words?

49268, 86394, 49468, ?

What 5 digit number continues the sequence?

A SUPER BAKE is an anagram of which two words that are similar in meaning?

Clue: breathing space

Which word in brackets is most opposite in meaning to the word in capitals?

ACQUIESCE (relinquish, bicker, renounce, achieve, conceive)

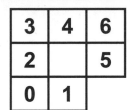

Which is the missing section?

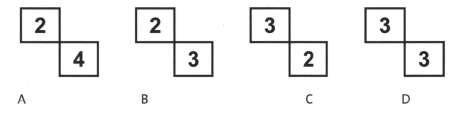

A   B   C   D

Start at one of the four corner letters and spiral clockwise round the perimeter, finishing at the centre letter to spell out a nine-letter word. You must provide the missing letters.

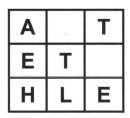

trachea is to windpipe as velum is to: palate, throat, mouth, membrane, voice

Which one of the following is not an anagram of a type of drink?

CHANGE MAP   MINI RAT

                          CAN PEAK

DONE MEAL   KEY WISH

659 : 21

983 : 69

749 : 19

687 : ??

Which two words are most opposite in meaning?

change, taint, cheapen, purify, redress, allow

17, 34, 102, 204, 612, 1224, ?

What number should replace the question mark?

What do the words; late, lease, added, raise and utter all have in common?

Look into some bodies and you will see little yellow-like flowers, usually of a colour thread, standing round in a ring.

Change the position of five words only in the above sentence so that it makes complete sense.

Which is the odd one out?

gazpacho, chowder, potage, brioche, vichyssoise

Only one group of 5 letters below can be re-arranged to spell out a 5-letter word in the English language. Identify the word.

IATDB   AOMKC   UBAQL

EATLH   ISZOR   IDCUT

1, 1000, 10.5, 905, 20, 810, 29.5, 715, ?, ?

What are the next two numbers in the above sequence?

What commonality is shared by the words flash, sad, dash, flags, half, gash, ask and lad?

A familiar phrase has had its initial letters and word boundaries removed. All remaining letters are in the correct order. What is the phrase?

UTOWNOIZE

What number should replace the question mark?

7	3	8	1	6
8	6	9	8	2
7	4	1	2	?
	7		5	

PINT
WAGE
HALF
IDOL
OPUS

What word comes next?

link, vary, unit, self or type ?

Which one of the following is not an anagram of an occupation?

SCARY TREE   RUM PLEB

CAME INCH

COARSEST   I BAN A CUTIE

20	17	16	13	12	9
19	16	15	12	11	8
16	13	12	9	8	
15	12	11	8		4
12				4	1
11	8	7	4	3	0

Which is the missing section?

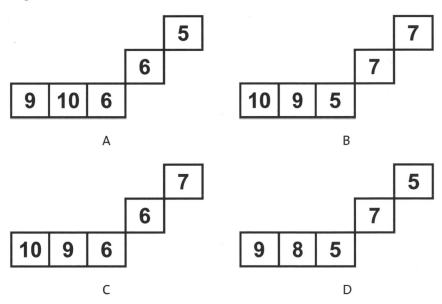

A

B

C

D

Combine three of the ten bits below to produce a word meaning: CLEMENT

ate, ard, pit, con, red, ute, dit, tem, ter, per

A man places a bookmark in a book. It is either between pages 100 and 101, 223 and 224 or 209 and 210.

Between which two pages is the bookmark?

A man walks 2 miles south, then 1 mile west, then 1 mile north, then 3 miles east, then 1 mile north.

How far away and in what direction is he from his original starting point?

inaugurate is to introduce as innovate is to: pioneer, actuate, commence, produce, germinate.

BOND HAS PAIN is an anagram of what familiar phrase?

Clue: man the lifeboats!

A   B   C   D   E   F   G   H

What letter is two to the right of the letter that comes midway between the letter four to the left of the letter F and the letter three to the right of the letter A ?

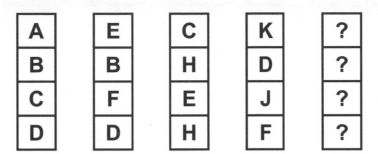

What letters should replace the question marks in the final column?

If Tony gives David £12.00, the money they have is in the ratio 2 : 1, however, if David gives Tony £2.00 the ratio is 1 : 3.

How much money have Tony and David each before they exchange any money?

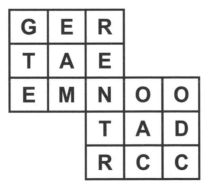

Each square contains the letters of a 9-letter word. Find the two words that are synonyms.

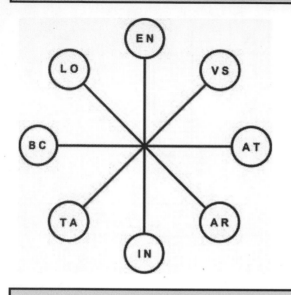

Find two 8 letter words reading clockwise that are antonyms.

Each word starts in a different circle and all letters are in the correct order.

What number is missing?

2	6		5	5		8	4
1	9		5	6		9	?

What two letters are missing from the sequence below?

wt, to, ls, ae, ??, fm, te, se, bw

Change one letter only in each of the words below to produce a familiar phrase.

RAN AID WIRE

Which is the odd one out?

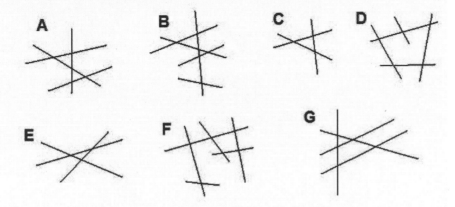

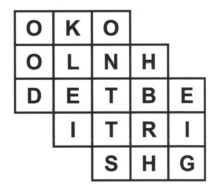

Find the starting point and work from letter to adjacent letter horizontally, vertically and diagonally to spell out a 19-letter phrase.

Every letter is used once each only.

Clue: keep your chin up

Place a word in the brackets that has the same meaning as the definitions either side of the brackets.

beloved   (   )   expensive

6 8 2 9 6 4 3 7 8 5 8

What is the difference between the average of the numbers above less the second lowest odd number?

Which is the odd one out?

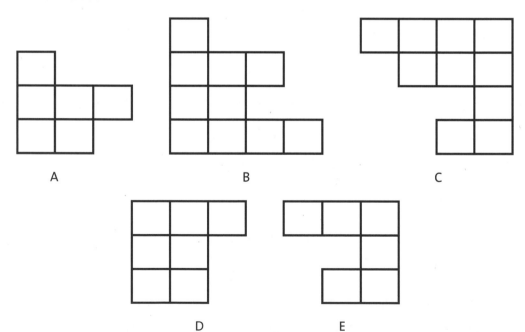

A   B   C

D   E

Which word in brackets is closest in meaning to the word in capitals?

AUDACIOUS (romantic, veritable, doughty, parsimonious, granular)

1	10	6	16
8	14	3	9
15	5	12	11
2	4	13	7

Swap round the position of three of the numbers only in the grid so that each row, column and corner to corner diagonal totals 34.

Add a letter to the beginning and end of an incline to make things moderately cold.

Place two letters in each set of brackets so that they produce a word when tacked onto the two letters to the left and another word when placed in front of the letters on the right.

The correct four sets of letters when read downwards in pairs will produce an 8-letter word.

WI (**) ST
CO(**) SK
MI (**) AR
FO (**) AS

9, 17, 12, 14, 15, 11, 18, ?, ?

What two numbers continue this sequence?

Which is the odd one out?

fitting, atypical, proper, expected, normal

What word can be placed in the brackets so that it forms another word or phrase when tacked onto the end of the first word, and another word or phrase when placed in front of the second word?

ram   (   )   ridge

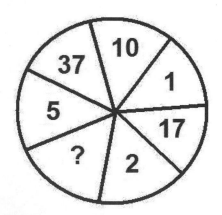

What number should replace the question mark?

Use each letter of the phrase below once each only to spell out three types of bear.

RAW PLAN AND A BOOK

Which two words are closest in meaning?

repository, alcove, receptacle, theatre, gargoyle, chamber

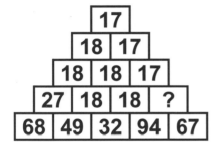

What number should replace the question mark?

DID TRUCE is an anagram of two this and that words, CUT, DRIED (cut and dried).

THUG MOB RULE is an anagram of which two other this and that words?

1469, 3271, 4693, 2714, ?

What four figure number comes next in the above sequence?

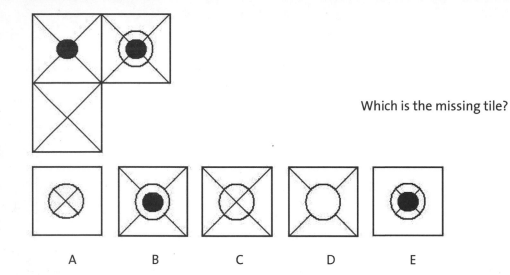

Which is the missing tile?

A B C D E

Solve the anagram of the 11- letter word in brackets to correctly complete the quotation by J.K.Galbraith.

If all else fails, immortality can always be assured by (PALACE CRUST) error.

5	2	6	7	29
3	1	5	9	16
8	5	3	8	25
7	3	2	9	?

What number should replace the question mark?

Add a letter to the beginning and end of radiance to make capricious.

C T M R N

What letter can be added several times to the above letters to produce a single word?

Place two letters in each set of brackets so that they produce a word when tacked onto the two letters to the left and another word when placed in front of the letters on the right.

The correct four sets of letters when read downwards in pairs will produce an 8-letter word.

LE (**) EW
LA(**) LL
DU (**) AR
DO (**) AL

My house is the third house from one end of my side of the street and the eleventh house away from the other end of my side of the street. How many houses are there on my side of the street?

propose is to contemplate as implement is to: plan, tool, design, execute, build

If 9 L of a C is Nine Lives of a Cat, what is represented by the following?

3 L on a T

16, 18, 22, 28, 30, 34, 40, ?

What number should replace the question mark to continue the sequence?

Which word in brackets is most similar in meaning to the word in capitals?

MALADROIT (disgruntled, awkward, neurotic, sarcastic, hurtful)

What is the missing number?

7214	56
3219	54
7322	?

In the course of a 5-day week a commuter spends £3.34 per day on bus fares and £4.62 per day on tube fares. How much money would she save per week if she bought a weekly combined bus and tube pass for £28.95, and how much would she save or lose if one week she takes two days off work due to illness and doesn't use her pass?

What single letter can be inserted into each of these words to form six new words?

rage, gash, area, beds, sack, taut

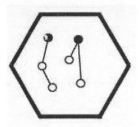

Which hexagon below has most in common with the hexagon above?

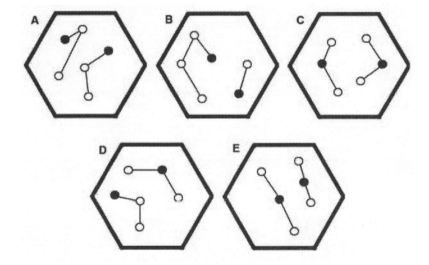

What word can be placed in the brackets so that it forms another word or phrase when tacked onto the end of the first word, and another word or phrase when placed in front of the second word?

night   (   )   rice

Solve the anagram of the 12-letter word in brackets to correctly complete the quotation by Harry S. Truman.

     When you have efficient government you have a (DISPATCH RIOT).

Change one letter only in each word below to form a familiar phrase.

LAD GOWN SHE SAW

Three of the ten bits below can be combined to spell out a 9 –letter word meaning ascertain. Find the word.

ina, erm, ant, det, ash, ine, tpr, ice, end, fis

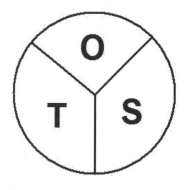 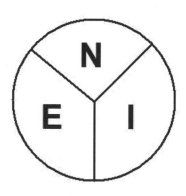 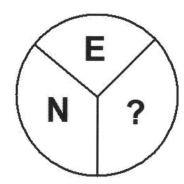

What letter should replace the question mark?

backbone is to determination as stamina is to: power, endurance, flair, brawn, courage

An electrical circuit wiring two sets of lights depends on a system of switches A, B, C and D. Each switch when working has the following effect on a set of lights:

Switch A turns lights 1 and 2 on/off or off/on

Switch B turns lights 2 and 4 on/off or off/on

Switch C turns lights 1 and 3 on/off or off/on

Switch D turns lights 3 and 4 on/off or off/on

 ON

 OFF

In the following, switches C, A, D, B are thrown in turn, with the result that Fig 1 is transformed into Fig 2. One of the switches is not, therefore, working and has had no effect on the numbered lights.

Identify which one of the switches is not working.

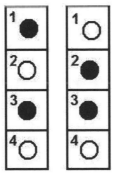

Fig. 1   Fig. 2

Place a word in the brackets that has the same meaning as the definitions either side of the brackets.

disturbance   (   )   abrade

6527

5692

8631

7138

5216

Which two numbers,
one on the right and
one on the left, are the
odd ones out?

6135

7625

9526

6138

1783

63219   is to   9210

and   59784   is to   14712

and   74354   is to   1139

therefore   28977   is to   ?

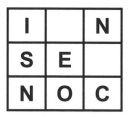

Start at one of the four corner letters and spiral clockwise round the perimeter, finishing at the centre letter to spell out a nine-letter word. You must provide the missing letters.

A well-known phrase has had its initial letters and word boundaries removed. What is the phrase?

ENDNAR

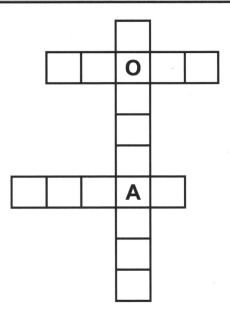

Insert the remaining letters below into the grid to find three related words.

UMYS   GTNM
TNIS   REK

9, 4, 12, 6, 18, 10, 21, 12, ? , ?

Which two numbers come next in the above sequence?

DID TRUCE is an anagram of two this and that words, CUT, DRIED (cut and dried).

FLOOD NUTS is an anagram of which two other this and that words?

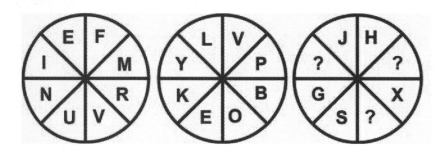

What letters should replace the question marks?

3 7 8 2 9 1 5 2 8 6 3 4 9 6 8

Delete all the numbers that appear more than once in the above list and then total up the remaining numbers. What are you left with?

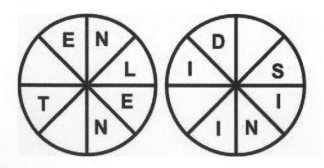

Find two 8-letter words, one reading clockwise round one circle and one reading anti-clockwise round the other circle, that are antonyms. You must provide the missing letters.

Which of the following is not an anagram of a boat or ship?

LONG ADO   SET VEER   GET FAIR
LEAN LOG   SEA TERM

What number is missing?

375	62830	246
263	24212	174
359	?	392

What comes next?

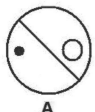 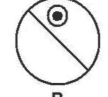 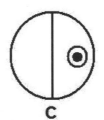  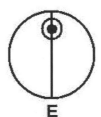

A   B   C   D   E

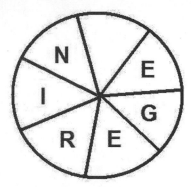

Find a 7-letter word reading clockwise. You must find the starting point and provide the missing letter.

The clue **mariners' garment makers** leads to what pair of rhyming words?

She did not ***** the ***** of *****, for she said that when she ***** the ***** of that ***** *****, she was ***** no ***** than her *****.

Insert the following ten words correctly into the above passage.

braved, doing, sea, praise, perils, stormy, more, feel, duty, need.

Which is the odd one out?

forsake, disclaim, abandon, abnegate, capitulate.

Which of the following is not an anagram of a sea-going vessel?

SEMI URBAN

                 HABIT SLEPT

GET FAIR

CURRIES

HOTEL PRICE

My watch was correct at midnight after which it began to lose 12 minutes per hour, until 5 hours ago it stopped completely. It now shows the time as 4.48. What is the correct time now?

Which two words are most opposite in meaning?

lively, susceptible, indifferent, unhappy, concerned, candid

What number should replace the question mark?

```
         14                          26

         75                         104
12                31           91         32

                      16

                       ?

             14           62
```

Start at one of the four corner letters and spiral clockwise round the perimeter, finishing at the centre letter, to spell out a nine-letter word. You must provide the missing letters.

What number should replace the question mark?

```
          71                        34
   56             28        12             16
          29                        17


                    93
             27            54
                    ?
```

4	1	6	3	7	4	9
7	5	2	2	9	7	4
5	4	1	4	9	?	5

What number should replace the question mark?

DID TRUCE is an anagram of two this and that words, CUT, DRIED (cut and dried).

NEAR OVEN is an anagram of which two other this and that words?

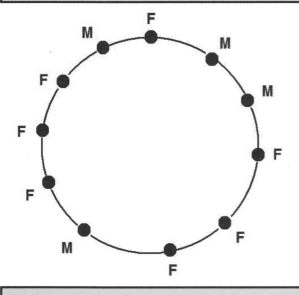

At this round table M = male and F = female.

How many people are sitting next to a male?

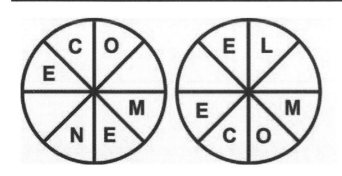

Find two 8-letter words, one reading clockwise around one circle and one reading anti-clockwise around the other circle, that are antonyms. You must provide the missing letters.

An electrical circuit wiring two sets of lights depends on a system of switches A, B, C and D. Each switch when working has the following effect on a set of lights:

Switch A turns lights 1 and 2 on/off or off/on

Switch B turns lights 2 and 4 on/off or off/on

Switch C turns lights 1 and 3 on/off or off/on

Switch D turns lights 3 and 4 on/off or off/on

 ON

 OFF

In the following, switches B, C, A, D are thrown in turn, with the result that Fig 1 is transformed into Fig 2. One of the switches is not, therefore, working and has had no effect on the numbered lights.

Identify which one of the switches is not working.

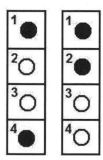

Fig. 1   Fig. 2

Which word is missing from the bracket?

POSE   (EPISODE)   PIED

MARE   (   )   DIET

You have 55 cubic blocks. What is the minimum number that need to be taken away in order to construct a solid cube with none left over?

A well-known phrase has had its initial letters and word boundaries removed. What is the phrase?

UTNOLD

Swap the position of five words in the sentence below so that it makes sense.

Parrots have a box jaw, and the upper bill is hooked, like a hinged-lid.

Put the following words into alphabetical order.

anarchism, analogize, analgesia, anatomist, anabolism, analysand, analogous, anaerobic, anatomize, analgesic, anarchist

Which of the following is not an anagram of a US state?

LEWD AREA

SAW NOTHING

NO OGRE

GUY SNEER

MADLY RAN

Test Nine: Question 14

Which is the odd one out?

comatose, peaceful, inactive, latent, torpid

Test Nine: Question 15

24	98	73	15
87	31	52	49
75	62	18	34
21	83	47	?

What number should replace the question mark?

Test Nine: Question 16

TU is to WV

and ABC is to FED

therefore OPQR is to ????

Test Nine: Question 17

1, 3, 6, 18, 36, 108, 216, ?

What number should replace the question mark to continue the sequence?

Test Nine: Question 18

What is the longest word that can be produced from the following ten letters?

NURDESBOTA

What number should replace the question mark?

5 6 3   4 7 **?**
2 8 4   2 8 6
8 4 7   7 6 5

Change one letter only in each word below to form a familiar phrase.

ROD SANE TIE RING

In a consignment of eggs 330 were cracked which was 15% of the total number of eggs. How many eggs were in the consignment?

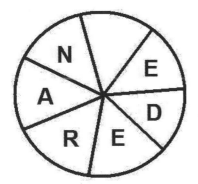

Find a seven letter word reading clockwise. You must provide the missing letter.

PEERS MEET SECT is an anagram of which two words that are similar in meaning?

1, 2 ¾, ? , 6 ¼ , 8

What number should replace the question mark?

feline is to cat as cervine is to: deer, cattle, goat, frog, squirrel

0, 100, 5.5, 94.5, 11, 89, 16.5, 83.5, ? , ?

What numbers should replace the question marks?

| culture | custard | winch |
| haven | full | grow |

What do all the above words have in common, and which one word below shares the same feature with them?

passage, luck, kind, money, chant

Which two words are closest in meaning?

extravagance, ostracism, vacillation, banishment, effusion, reticence

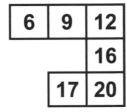

Which is the missing section?

A   B   C   D

What three letter word can be placed in the brackets so that it completes two words on the left and starts two words on the right?

CH   IST

(   )

QU   ERY

What word can be placed in the brackets so that it forms another word or phrase when tacked onto the end of the first word, and another word or phrase when placed in front of the second word?

sea　　　　(　　　　)　　　　mark

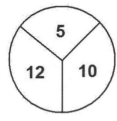 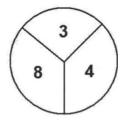 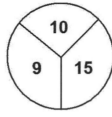 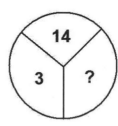

What number should replace the question mark?

Which two words are most opposite in meaning?

tender, mock, uneven, real, alien, offbeat

What number should replace the question mark?

38	16	72	11	61
10				18
67				86
?				8
16	8	**39**	16	**41**

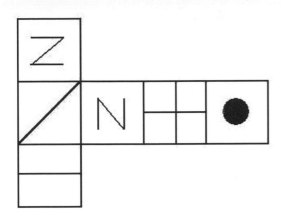

When the above is folded to form a cube, which is the only one of the following that can be produced?

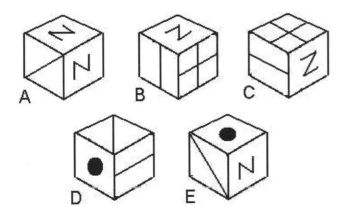

Three of the ten bits below can be combined to spell out a word meaning principle. What is the word?

ale, ant, car, ess, ion, nic, ric, rat, ler, phe

curt is to abrupt as cursory is to: expeditious, perfunctory, alacrity, summary, celerity

Place a word in the brackets that has the same meaning as the definitions either side of the brackets.

toss　　　　　(　　)　　　　　bitumen

If 1 = G. T. D. A represents the familiar phrase: one good turn deserves another, what familiar phrase is represented by:

1 = M. M. is A. M. P

Which number is the odd one out?

4379　　　　63915　　　　2579

45913　　　　81917　　　　43711

I travel to work by bus and train. If my bus journey takes 37 minutes and my train journey takes 15 minutes longer, what is the total travelling time in hours and minutes?

What pair of letters do not appear in the sequence below?

lo, es, ue, he, ua, en, eb, el

Which of the following is not an anagram of an element?

SNUG TENT   NO CRAB

TULIP MAN

IMMUNE GAS   ARC A MOON

Which word in brackets is closest in meaning to the word in capitals?

INTERPRET (appraise, construe, punctuate, imply, inspirit)

In the phrase below the first letter of each word has been removed as well as spacing. What is the phrase?

CTOURGE

TORE, SOLID, UNIT, RAISE, ALE, DINE, TREE, ?

What comes next?

ROUT, SEAL, USED, POUND, SPARE

What word can be placed in the brackets so that it forms another word or phrase when tacked onto the end of the first word, and another word or phrase when placed in front of the second word?

back   (   )   suit

3.7, 7.4, 11.1, 14.8, ?

What number should replace the question mark to continue the sequence?

Find two eight letters words, one in each circle and both reading anti-clockwise, that are antonyms. You must provide the missing letters.

25	21	17	13	12	11
24	20	16	12	11	10
23	19		11	10	9
22		14		9	8
18	14	10		5	4
14	10		2	1	0

Which is the missing section?

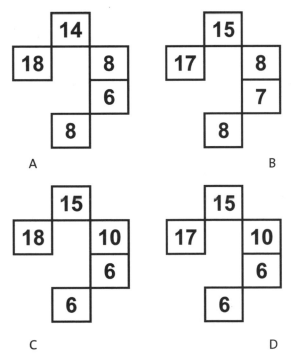

A

B

C

D

A well-known phrase has had its initial letters and word boundaries removed. What is the phrase?

IPNHEUD

In a game of fourteen players lasting for 80 minutes, six substitutes alternate equally with each player. This means that all players including the substitutes are on the pitch for the same length of time. For how long?

assign is to delegate as assignment is to: vocation, duty, quota, perform, commission

Use every letter of the phrase REGIMENT MARCH once each only to spell out three units of measurement.

What number is missing from the third bracket?

```
25  (149)  97
31  (611)  58
29  ( ? )  64
```

Which word in brackets is closest in meaning to the word in capitals?

CONVENTION (dialogue, apparel, seminar, semester, sequence)

Which of the following is not an anagram of a plant?

THE HARE   COB COAT

                              BARE TOP

AIR PLUM   HE TILTS

What is the longest word in the English language that can be produced from the ten letters below? No letter may be used more than once.

AMTPKLFOJC

Which word below is in the wrong column?

Column A   Column B

bird   hot
list   wash
board   smith
guard   ant
mail   lie
                  bait

Which is the odd one out?

exist, abide, mania, estop, thief, realm, laugh

BATHE HARDY NAG is an anagram of what familiar phrase (4, 2, 1, 6 letters long)?

Clue: precarious

Which word in brackets is most similar in meaning to the word in capitals?

REBUT (negate, withdraw, decline, disclaim, reiterate)

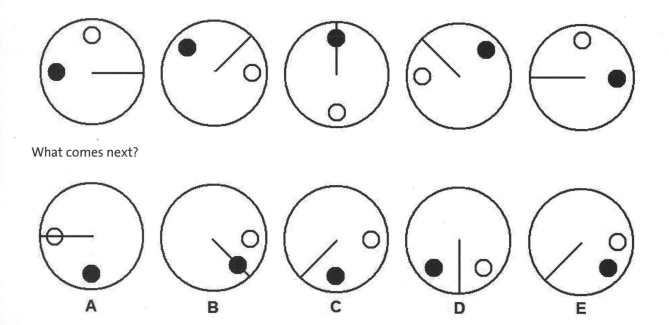

What comes next?

A   B   C   D   E

* A X N * * *

Complete the above word meaning negligence.

DID TRUCE is an anagram of two this and that words, CUT, DRIED (cut and dried).

OFFER KINK is an anagram of which two other this and that words?

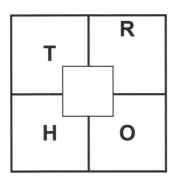 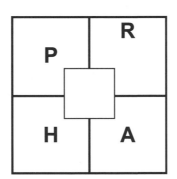 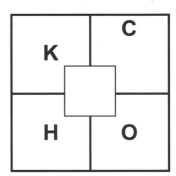

The same letter is missing from the centre of each square. What is the letter?

In my fish tank I have 12 measle fish. The male fish have 42 spots each and the female fish have 14 spots each.

If I transfer two thirds of the male fish to another tank, how many spots do the fish that now remain in the original tank have between them?

Spell out a 12-letter word by moving from letter to adjacent letter vertically and horizontally, but not diagonally. You must provide the missing letters.

Which word in brackets is closest in meaning to the word in capitals?

SPROCKET (thread, hole, plug, cog, device)

What is the missing number?

22	19		62	27		36	38
	3			7			?
7	14		15	22		24	34

Insert a mythical Greek character onto the bottom line to complete eight 3-letter words reading downwards.

A	T	F	A	Y	P	H	W
S	O	A	R	O	A	O	A
*	*	*	*	*	*	*	*

Three of the ten bits below can be combined to spell out a word meaning dynamo. What is the word?

sto, ula, ist, tor, era, ndo, mal, esh, gen, art

Place two letters in each set of brackets so that they produce a word when tacked onto the two letters to the left and another word when placed in front of the letters on the right.

The correct four sets of letters when read downwards in pairs will produce an 8-letter word.

BA (**) AL
BI (**) HY
NE (**) US
CO (**) AS

Which is the odd one out?

enunciate, chant, articulate, utter, pronounce

Place a word in the brackets that has the same meaning as the definitions either side of the brackets.

more level   (   )   complement

1000, 983, 949, 898, 830, 745, ?

What number should replace the question mark?

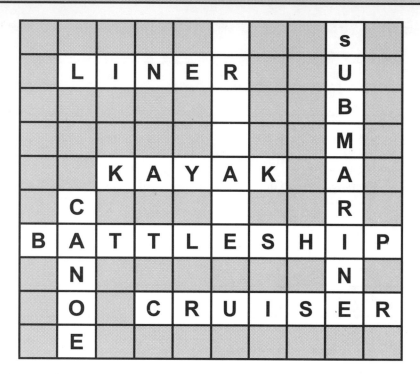

Complete the missing word

What number is missing from the bottom right-hand corner?

3	9	1	7
4	5	6	7
6	6	4	4
1	8	3	?

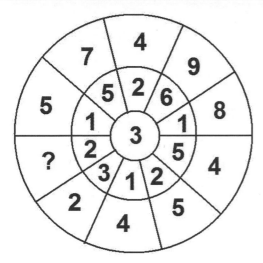

What number should replace the question mark?

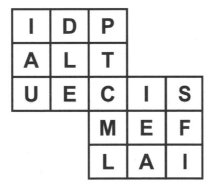

Each square contains the letters of a 9-letter word. Find the two words that are synonyms.

Test One Answer 1

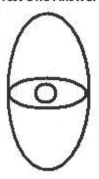

The ellipse alternates horizontal/vertical and the dot alternates black/white

Test One Answer 2
D: lines across progress +2, +3, +4; lines down progress +4, +3, +2

Test One Answer 3
Jim 36, Sid 54, Alf 81

Test One Answer 4
immobile, vigorous

Test One Answer 5
F   K

AbCdeFgHijKlMnoPqRstUvWxyZ

Test One Answer 6
plot

Test One Answer 7
The elephants in the zoo looked very old and dusty, as though they had worn their skins too long, and needed new ones.

Test One Answer 8
e. medieval crossbow

Test One Answer 9
D: the symbol top left moves to bottom right, the symbol top right moves to top left, the symbol bottom right moves to bottom left.

Test One Answer 10
23 : start at 5736942 and working anti-clockwise, reverse the previous number and discard the largest digit

Test One Answer 11
crude, genteel

Test One Answer 12
actually, indeed

Test One Answer 13
5: add 1 ¾ each time

Test One Answer 14
a tidal man = Dalmatian

The birds are;
Pheasant (heat pans)
Pelican (a pencil)
Pigeon (one pig)
Condor (cordon)

Test One Answer 15
unbelievable

Test One Answer 16
veer, gyrate

Test One Answer 17
Faith £36
Hope £24
Charity £12

Test One Answer 18
more often than not

Test One Answer 19
B: add the number of white dots then change them to black in the final square. Likewise, add the number of black dots and change them to white.

Test One Answer 20
8245:
79 + 3 (**36**) = 82 and 36 + 9 (**79**) = 45

Test One Answer 21
maternal, motherly

Test One Answer 22
60%

Total age = 400
Average age = 40 (400 ÷ 10)
Number of people less than 40 is 6 = 60%

Test One Answer 23
UCLDI = lucid

Test One Answer 24
aorta: it is in the heart. The rest are in the brain.

Test One Answer 25
6
spot, post, stop, tops, opts, pots

Test One Answer 26
therapeutic: it contains the word ape in forward order – ther**ape**utic.

The rest contain animals in reverse order :
mous**tac**he (cat), pa**god**a (dog), fran**gip**ane (pig), volun**tary** (rat)

Test One Answer 27
NMKJ:
ZYxWVuTSrQPoNMlKJ

Test One Answer 28
38:
Take the numbers at the bottom of each pyramid as follows in order to produce the number at the top:

9 ÷ 3 = 3 and 8 x 1 = 8

Similarly 8 ÷ 2 = 4 and 4 x 2 = 8
6 ÷ 3 = 2 and 3 x 3 = 9

Test One Answer 29
E: so that each connected straight line of three squares contains five black dots and four white dots.

Test One Answer 30
give a leg up

Test One Answer 31
take the bull by the horns

Test One Answer 32
ground

Test One Answer 33
Tom	£168
Dick	£189
Harry	£63
	£420

Test One Answer 34
turn: over turn, turn-coat

Test One Answer 35
sacred

Test One Answer 36
switch C is faulty

Test One Answer 37
34
The numbers indicate the crosses in the same line across and down.

Test One Answer 38
1 :
5 x 9 = 45,
6 x 8 = 48
3 x 7 = 21

Test One Answer 39
wrong gong

Test One Answer 40
every picture tells a story.

Test Two: Solutions

Test Two Answer 1

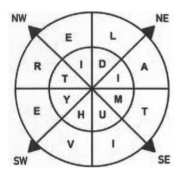

relative humidity

Test Two Answer 2
12:
$(8 + 9 + 7) \div 2$

Test Two Answer 3
as far as one can tell

Test Two Answer 4
drill

Test Two Answer 5
1
In each line across and down, the sum of the first and third digits equals the sum of the second and fourth digits.

Test Two Answer 6
red
They are all words which appear in turn in the word SPARED: (spa)red, s(pare)d, sp(are)d, spa(red)

Test Two Answer 7
C: lines across progress +1, +2, +3, +4 in turn; lines down progress +4, +5, +6, +7 in turn.

Test Two Answer 8
wolf.
Pair the words to produce tapeworm, headroom, password and werewolf.

Test Two Answer 9
4 girls and 3 boys

Test Two Answer 10
TADIM = admit

Test Two Answer 11
543:
x 2 + 1 each time

Test Two Answer 12
guileless

Test Two Answer 13
21040; 4 x 5260 = 21040

Test Two Answer 14
Waywardly

Test Two Answer 15
64613 and 75924

Test Two Answer 16
a. to treat like a celebrity

Test Two Answer 17
fork handles
four candles

Test Two Answer 18
towering
towering means high, the rest mean broad

Test Two Answer 19
GIHJK: in all the others the third and fourth letters
are alphabetically reversed. In GIHJK the second and
third letters are reversed.

Test Two Answer 20
26
3 numbers 16 x 3 = 48
2 numbers 11 x 2 = 22

Therefore, third number is 48 – 22 = 26

Test Two Answer 21
humanely

Test Two Answer 22
connive, expedite

Test Two Answer 23
3 : each horizontal line contains the digits 1-9 once
each only

Test Two Answer 24
D: the contents of the third square in each line are
the combined contents of the first two squares.

Test Two Answer 25
7312468
The second number consists of the odd numbers
from the first number in descending order followed
by the even numbers in ascending order.

Test Two Answer 26

Add a new dot, alternating black then white, at 45°
intervals working clockwise.

Test Two Answer 27
compromise

Test Two Answer 28

8	4	6	8
6	1	2	2
8	4		
4	6		

In each row of four squares across and down, the number formed by the second and fourth digits is the result of multiplying together the first and third digits, for example,
$8 \times 6 = 48$

Test Two Answer 29
deterrent, incentive

Test Two Answer 30
1 metre

1 metre (sapling) + 5 metres = 6 metres (fence)

Test Two Answer 31
B: A = E (5 lines) and C = D (6 lines)
B has only 4 lines

Test Two Answer 32
befitting.
Each word contains within it a synonym of the word it equals:

tol(era)nt = epoch
kno(win)gly = triumph
ener(get)ic = acquire
c(apt)ivate = befitting

Test Two Answer 33
run out of steam

Test Two Answer 34
flower

Test Two Answer 35
6

Test Two Answer 36
scratch, abrade

Test Two Answer 37
$21 : 7 \times 9 = 63 / 3 = 21$

Test Two Answer 38

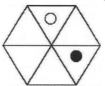

At each stage the white dot moves one segment clockwise, and the black dot moves two segments clockwise.

Test Two Answer 39
24 ; each number describes its position in the grid. 24 indicates column 2, row 4

Test Two Answer 40
Switch D is faulty

Test Three: Solutions

Test Three Answer 1
set: all words can be prefixed with SUN
sundry, sunlit, sunburn, sunflower, sunset

Test Three Answer 2
805, 360

There are two interwoven sequences: start at 100 and add 65, start at 1000 and deduct 65

Test Three Answer 3
levity: each word commences with the second and fifth letters of the previous word.

Test Three Answer 4
give a new lease of life

Test Three Answer 5
G

Test Three Answer 6
6:
multiply the numbers top and bottom to produce the number in the middle i.e. 7 x 9 = 63

Test Three Answer 7
petals, stalk

Test Three Answer 8
24
In each triangle; divide the top number by 2, the bottom left number by 3 and the bottom right number by 4. Then add the three resultant numbers to obtain the number in the middle.

Test Three Answer 9
C

Test Three Answer 10
c. relating to a deacon

Test Three Answer 11
constrict

Test Three Answer 12
640:
It is the four times table – 4, 8, 12, 16, 20, 24, 28, 32, 36, 40 – split into groups of 3 numbers.

Test Three Answer 13
prolix
It means long-winded. The rest mean brief

Test Three Answer 14
ONGYU = young

Test Three Answer 15
Transfer numbers from the first grid to the second grid by deducting 1 from the odd numbers, and adding 1 to the even numbers

6	5	2	3	4
7	9	4	2	9
5	4	6	3	8
7	2	4	6	9

Test Three Answer 16
get into shape

Test Three Answer 17
unlikely

Test Three Answer 18
A: Looking at lines across add 2 and 3 alternately. Looking down, add 3 and 2 alternately

Test Three Answer 19
league

Test Three Answer 20
15:      (15 + 7) x 6 = 132

Test Three Answer 21
government

Test Three Answer 22
grand slam to produce rag, far, sea, tan, cod, has, pal, pea and gem

Test Three Answer 23
repeated, unbroken

Test Three Answer 24
D: add the contents of the first two boxes to

produce the contents of the third box, however, only carry forward lines that appear in the same position in both boxes.

Test Three Answer 25
oscilloscope

Test Three Answer 26
C: Looking at lines across and down, each number is the sum of the previous two numbers.

Test Three Answer 27
refrain

Test Three Answer 28
jittery, calm

Test Three Answer 29
circumnavigation

Test Three Answer 30
2146: in all the others multiply the first and last digits to obtain the two middle digits

Test Three Answer 31
9:
14 + 13 = 27   27 ÷ 3 = 9
39 + 15 = 54   54 ÷ 6 = 9

Test Three Answer 32
The Old Curiosity Shop (anagram: the lousy chiropodist)

Test Three Answer 33
8: The numbers 2, 8, 6, 9, 7, 4, 3 appear reading clockwise in the same order around each heptagon.

Test Three Answer 34
Every picture tells a story

Test Three Answer 35
wind

Test Three Answer 36
Saturday

Test Three Answer 37
6:
Multiply the top left-hand number by the bottom right-hand number to obtain the number formed by the bottom left-hand and top right-hand digits.

Test Three Answer 38
zephyr, wind

Test Three Answer 39
547
326

The numbers move in the pattern:
ABC   BFD
DEF   to   ECA

Test Three Answer 40
C: the rest are all the same figure rotated.

Test Four: Solutions

Test Four Answer 1
thieve, vendor, origin, income, meddle, length

Test Four Answer 2
4:

The right hand pairs of digits each form a number that is double the left-hand pairs of digits, albeit not in the same order. i.e. 39/78, 17/34, 46/92, 28/56

Test Four Answer 3
Temper

Test Four Answer 4
1 ½
3/4 ÷ ½ = ¾ x 2/1 = 6/4 = 3/2 = 1 ½

Test Four Answer 5
portable, compact

Test Four Answer 6
29: alternate numbers in each column add to 100

Test Four Answer 7
The year dot

Test Four Answer 8
13 kg (1, 3, 5, 7, 9, 11, 13)

Test Four Answer 9
as the case may be

Test Four Answer 10

	U			A			R	
Q	W	E	D	O				E
	M			H			I	
	E			E			F	
S		B	Y	A	N			N
	U			O			A	
	S			F			S	
R	O	X	G	O				U
	E			B			M	

square number

Test Four Answer 11
294

98 = 1/3, therefore, 196 (2 x 98) = 2/3 remaining.

Test Four Answer 12
because, that

Test Four Answer 13
VII   V   III   XII   IX

Test Four Answer 14
heaven on earth

Test Four Answer 15

Looking across the blocks of four, there are four sequences:

AbCdEfG

DefghIjklmNopqrS

BcdEfgHijK

CdefGhijKlmnO

Test Four Answer 16
11 ¼ days

5 men take 5 x 27 = 135 man days

12 men take 135 ÷ 12 = 11 ¼ days

Test Four Answer 17
cob, pen (male and female swan)

Test Four Answer 18
48:    6 x 4 = 24 (x 2) = 48
        7 + 5 = 12 (x 4) = 48

Test Four Answer 19
B: lines are carried forward from the first two hexagons to the final hexagon, except when two lines appear in the same position, in which case they are cancelled out.

Test Four Answer 20
Sunday:
Miss 1, 2, 3, 4, 5 days in turn

Test Four Answer 21
launch

Test Four Answer 22
Spruce

Test Four Answer 23
annoyance

Test Four Answer 24

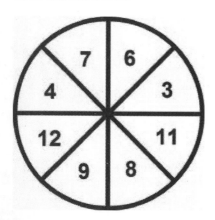

In the first circle, opposite segments total 9. In the second they total 11, in the third 13 and in the fourth 15.

Test Four Answer 25
archaic

Test Four Answer 26
dramatize:
It means to play up
The rest mean to play down.

Test Four Answer 27

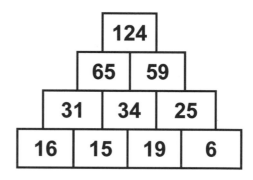

Test Four Answer 28
camp

Test Four Answer 29
17 minutes

12 noon less 17 minutes = 11.43
11.43 less 35 minutes = 11. 08
10 a.m. plus 68 minutes (17 x 4) = 11.08

Test Four Answer 30
paradise, bliss

Test Four Answer 31

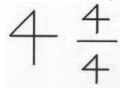

Test Four Answer 32
Estonia and England

Test Four Answer 33
Switch A is faulty

Test Four Answer 34
d. dialogue

Test Four Answer 35
R:
The words START and STOP are spelled out by
alternate letters.

Test Four Answer 36
Perspex

It is plastic
The rest are made of glass.

Test Four Answer 37
EINTL = inlet

Test Four Answer 38
8: the ones that form the inner 2x2x2 core

Test Four Answer 39
palatable, tasteless

Test Four Answer 40
C: numbers across progress +5, +2, +5; numbers
down progress +2, +5, +2

Test Five: Solutions

Test Five Answer 1
Rio Grande: to produce fir, lei, too, big, fur, tea, sin,
mad, bee

Test Five Answer 2
wick, filament

Test Five Answer 3
juvenile, youthful

Test Five Answer 4
run

Test Five Answer 5
67:
Combined age in 13 years time = 83
4 x 13 = 52, therefore, combined age now is 83 − 52
= 31.
In nine years time combined age is 31 + 36 (4 x 9) =
67

Test Five Answer 6
5:
the number in the middle is the average of the
numbers around the outside.

Test Five Answer 7
d. boasting

Test Five Answer 8
D: the circles are in identical pairs, albeit rotated.

Test Five Answer 9

T	3	6
4	7	2
1	5	8

Visit the squares in the above numbered order.

Test Five Answer 10
from time to time

Test Five Answer 11
OANJB = banjo

Test Five Answer 12
Bill 28, Ben 35

Test Five Answer 13
exultant, ecstatic

Test Five Answer 14
11:     39/13 = 3,   40/5 = 8,   3 + 8 = 11

Test Five Answer 15
B: looking across add a horizontal line to alternate squares. Looking down add a vertical line to alternate squares.

Test Five Answer 16
Practising what I preach

Test Five Answer 17

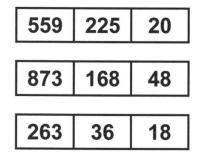

559	225	20
873	168	48
263	36	18

In each line multiply together the digits of each number to obtain the following number.

Test Five Answer 18
Weight

Test Five Answer 19
coach

Test Five Answer 20
philanthropic, penurious

Test Five Answer 21
WNW   SW   SSW   SSE   ESE   NE
NNE

Test Five Answer 22
Connected numbers are in the ratio 1 : 4. The connected pairs should, therefore, be 6.9/27.6 and 4.7/18.8

5.3 is the odd number left out.

Test Five Answer 23
A: Looking across and down each number is the sum of the previous two numbers.

Test Five Answer 24
eighths:
The letters ABCDEFGH appear as follows:

P L A C E B O
S E C L U D E
S P E C I F Y
E I G H T H S

Test Five Answer 25
ii. C
MEDICAL – MEDIAL

Test Five Answer 26
stock, cargo

Test Five Answer 27
architecture

Test Five Answer 28
172

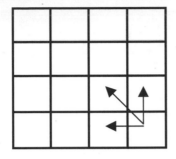

Each number is the sum of the three adjacent numbers as indicated by the arrows.

Test Five Answer 29
stable, shaky

Test Five Answer 30
-2.5: Deduct 3.5 each time

Test Five Answer 31
fiscal, monetary

Test Five Answer 32
Switch C is faulty

Test Five Answer 33
actions speak louder than words

Test Five Answer 34

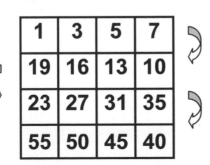

Work along the top line then back along the second line etc, as indicated, adding 2, 3, 4, 5

Test Five Answer 35
Frontispiece

Test Five Answer 36
H

AbcdEfgHiJklmNopQrStuvWxyZ

Test Five Answer 37
6   4
There are four sequences reading across the four boxes in the same position.

9, 7, 5, 3
0, 3, 6, 9
2, 4, 6, 8
6, 5, 4, 3

Test Five Answer 38

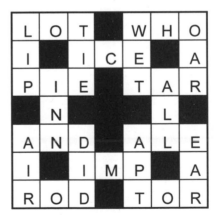

Test Five Answer 39
dagger, star

Test Five Answer 40
217 : 7 x 3 = 21, 5 + 2 = 7

Test Six Answer 1
5; looking across, the sum of each pair of numbers is one more than the previous pair of numbers

Test Six Answer 2
Putting all my eggs in one basket

Test Six Answer 3
TFG: The first letter moves forward two places in the alphabet, the second letter moves three back and the third letter moves three forward.

Test Six Answer 4
Saturday 20 May

Test Six Answer 5
9 Planets in the Solar System

Test Six Answer 6
impersonator

Test Six Answer 7
In 15 years

	-5	Now	+15
Matthew	40	45	60
Amy	10	15	30

Test Six Answer 8
manifest, apparent

Test Six Answer 9
7
7
9
9
Start at the bottom left-hand corner and work along the bottom row, then back along the row above etc., repeating the numbers 79364

Test Six Answer 10
Pack – the chemical symbols are pa = Pascal, c = Coulomb, k = Kelvin

Test Six Answer 11
emanate (or manatee)

Test Six Answer 12
half measures (acre, degree, micron, kilogram, centimetre, mile, volt, ampere)

Test Six Answer 13
Halloween.
Lone whale is an anagram of Halloween, and trims cash is an anagram of Christmas

Test Six Answer 14
rotate, swing (on a clock the hands rotate and a pendulum swings)

Test Six Answer 15
test

Test Six Answer 16
D: the square rotates $45°$ clockwise at each stage and the dot alternates white/black.

Test Six Answer 17
PQR
ABCdEFGhiJKLmnoPQRstuvWXY

Test Six Answer 18
1

$72 \times 6/9 = 48$
1/3 of 48 = 16
12.5% of 16 = 2
½ of 2 = 1

Test Six Answer 19
entwine, unravel

Test Six Answer 20
4: each horizontal and vertical line of 4 numbers totals 18

Test Six Answer 21
tube

Test Six Answer 22
right byte

Test Six Answer 23
MELON
Each letter moves up 10 places in the alphabet.

Test Six Answer 24
black and white

Test Six Answer 25
86594
Reverse each number and add one to the middle digit to produce the next number in the sequence.

Test Six Answer 26
pause, break

Test Six Answer 27
bicker

Test Six Answer 28
D: Looking across add 1 then 2. looking down subtract 1 then 2.

Test Six Answer 29
heartfelt

Test Six Answer 30
Palate

Test Six Answer 31
CAN PEAK = pancake.
The drinks are: champagne (change map), lemonade (done meal), martini (mini rat) and whiskey (key wish)

Test Six Answer 32
41: (6 x 8)-7

Test Six Answer 33
taint, purify

Test Six Answer 34
3672: multiply by 2 then 3 alternately

Test Six Answer 35
They can be prefixed with P to form another word: plate, please, padded, praise, putter

Test Six Answer 36
Look into some flowers and you will see little thread-like bodies, usually of a yellow colour, standing round in a ring.

Test Six Answer 37
brioche: it is bread
The rest are soups

Test Six Answer 38
EATLH = lathe

Test Six Answer 39
39, 620

there are two interwoven sequences. Add 9.5 starting at 1, and subtract 95 starting at 1000

Test Six Answer 40
They can all be typed on the middle row of a QWERTY keyboard (asdfghjkl)

Test Seven Answer 1
cut down to size

Test Seven Answer 2
6; respective columns total 22, 20, 18, 16, 14

Test Seven Answer 3
VARY. Each word commences with the letter that comes three places in the alphabet after the last letter of the previous word, for example: PINT uv WAGE fg HALF etc

Test Seven Answer 4
COARSEST = Socrates
The occupations are: secretary (scary tree), mechanic (came inch), plumber (rum pleb), beautician (I ban a cutie)

Test Seven Answer 5
D: lines across progress -3, -1, -3, -1, -3; lines down progress -1, -3, -1, -3, -1.

Test Seven Answer 6
temperate

Test Seven Answer 7
Between 100 and 101.
The other numbers are on opposite sides of the same page.

Test Seven Answer 8
2 miles east

Test Seven Answer 9
Pioneer

Test Seven Answer 10
abandon ship

Test Seven Answer 11
E

Test Seven Answer 12

There are four sequences as indicated by the lines:
ABCDE
BcdEfgHijKlmN
CDEFG
DeFgHiJkL

Test Seven Answer 13
Tony £124, David £44

124 − 12 = 112	124 + 2 = 126
44 + 12 = 56	44 − 2 = 42

Test Seven Answer 14
agreement, concordat

Test Seven Answer 15
variable, constant

Test Seven Answer 16
3: Looking across numbers in the same position in each set of 4, there are four series:
2 5 8 (increase by 3)
6 5 4 (reduce by 1)
1 5 9 (increase by 4)
9 6 3 (reduce by 3)

Test Seven Answer 17
mg: it is a list of the first and last letters from each word in the question.

Test Seven Answer 18
man and wife

Test Seven Answer 19
F: It has 6 lines

A and G have four lines each, B and D have five, C and E have three.

Test Seven Answer 20
look on the bright side

Test Seven Answer 21
dear

Test Seven Answer 22
1
Average = 6, lowest odd number = 5

Test Seven Answer 23
D: A + C and B + E combine to construct 4 x 4 square grids.

Test Seven Answer 24
doughty

Test Seven Answer 25

1	11	6	16
8	14	3	9
15	5	12	2
10	4	13	7

Test Seven Answer 26
Hill – chilly

Test Seven Answer 27
pedestal: wipe/pest, code/desk, mist/star, foal/alas

Test Seven Answer 28
8, 21

There are two interwoven sequences. Start at 9 and add 3. Start at 17 and subtract 3.

Test Seven Answer 29
atypical
It means out of character
The rest mean as expected or in character.

Test Seven Answer 30
part

Test Seven Answer 31
26: Start at 1 and, working clockwise, jump to alternate segments adding 1, 3, 5, 7, 9, 11

Test Seven Answer 32
koala, panda, brown

Test Seven Answer 33
repository, receptacle

Test Seven Answer 34
26: each number is arrived at by adding the four digits of the two numbers immediately below it, i.e. 9 + 4 + 6 + 7 = 26

Test Seven Answer 35
rough and tumble

Test Seven Answer 36
6932: the numbers 1469327 are being repeated in groups of 4

Test Seven Answer 37
C: looking across a large circle is added. Looking down the black circle disappears.

Test Seven Answer 38
spectacular

Test Seven Answer 39
33 : in each line take the difference between numbers formed by alternate digits;
72 - 39 = 33

Test Seven Answer 40
Light – flighty

Test Eight

Solutions

Test Eight Answer 1
The letter A; to produce catamaran.

Test Eight Answer 2
ancestor: to produce lean/anew, lace/cell, dust/star, door/oral

Test Eight Answer 3
13
```
     *
__ _ _ _ _ _ _ _ _ _ _
```

Test Eight Answer 4
execute

Test Eight Answer 5
3 legs on a tripod

Test Eight Answer 6
42: +2, +4, +6 repeated

Test Eight Answer 7
awkward

Test Eight Answer 8
84 : 7 x 3 x 2 x 2

Test Eight Answer 9
a) save £10.85
b) lose £5.07

Test Eight Answer 10
N to produce; range, gnash, arena, bends, snack, taunt

Test Eight Answer 11
D: it contains the same two strings;
black/white/white and white/black/white

Test Eight Answer 12
Cap: nightcap, caprice

Test Eight Answer 13
dictatorship

Test Eight Answer 14
Lay down the law

Test Eight Answer 15
determine

Test Eight Answer 16
X: the words in each circle then spell: ONE, TEN, SIX, reading letters in the same segments.

Test Eight Answer 17
endurance

Test Eight Answer 18
Switch A is faulty

Test Eight Answer 19
fray

Test Eight Answer 20
5216 and 6135:
The rest are in anagram pairs: 5692/9526,
7138/1783, 6527/7625, 8631/6138

Test Eight Answer 21
10914:
(2 + 8) (9) (7 + 7)

Test Eight Answer 22
consignee

Test Eight Answer 23
lend an ear (or bend an ear)

Test Eight Answer 24

Test Eight Answer 25
27,16

There are two interwoven sequences: start at 9 and
add 3, 6, 3. Start at 4 and add 2, 4, 2.

Test Eight Answer 26
Lost and found

Test Eight Answer 27

Opposite letters are the same distance from the
beginning and end of the alphabet respectively.

Test Eight Answer 28
17 (7 + 1 + 5 + 4)

Test Eight Answer 29
lengthen, diminish

Test Eight Answer 30
SET VEER = EVEREST. The boats are gondola,
galleon, steamer and frigate

Test Eight Answer 31
94518: 3 x 3 = 9, 5 x 9 = 45, 9 x 2 = 18

Test Eight Answer 32
B: the circle moves top to bottom alternately. The line moves 45° clockwise. The black dot moves 45° clockwise.

Test Eight Answer 33
integer

Test Eight Answer 34
sailors' tailors

Test Eight Answer 35
She did not feel the need of praise, for she said that when she braved the perils of that stormy sea, she was doing no more than her duty.

Test Eight Answer 36
capitulate
It means to give in to. The rest mean to give up.

Test Eight Answer 37
HOTEL PRICE = helicopter.

The vessels are submarine (semi urban), cruiser (curries), battleship (habit slept), frigate (get fair)

Test Eight Answer 38
11 a.m.

midnight	=	midnight
1 a.m.	=	12.48
2 a.m.	=	1.36
3 a.m.	=	2.24
4 a.m.	=	3.12
5 a.m.	=	4.00
6 a.m.	=	4.48

+5 hours = 11 a.m.

Test Eight Answer 39
indifferent, concerned

Test Eight Answer 40
128; reverse each number and add to produce the number in the centre, i.e. 61 + 41 + 26 = 128

Test Nine: Solutions

Test Nine Answer 1
wonderful

Test Nine Answer 2
30 : it is the sum of all the digits above i.e. 9 + 3 + 2 + 7 + 5 + 4

Test Nine Answer 3
8: in each line add the fourth digit to each of the first three digits to produce the last three digits.

Test Nine Answer 4
ever and anon

Test Nine Answer 5
7 people

Test Nine Answer 6
commence, complete

Test Nine Answer 7
Switch B is faulty

Test Nine Answer 8

POSE	(EPISODE)	PIED
2 54 1	12345 6 7	376
MARE	(EMIRATE)	DIET

Test Nine Answer 9
28: the next cube number below 64 (4 x 4 x 4) is 27 (3 x 3 x 3). In order to construct a 3 x 3 x 3 solid cube, therefore, with none left over 55 − 27 = 28 blocks need to be taken away.

Test Nine Answer 10
put on hold

Test Nine Answer 11
Parrots have a hooked bill, and the upper jaw is hinged, like a box-lid.

Test Nine Answer 12
anabolism, anaerobic, analgesia, analgesic, analogize, analogous, analysand, anarchism, anarchist, anatomist, anatomize

Test Nine Answer 13
GUY SNEER = Guernsey. The US states are Delaware (lewd area), Oregon (no ogre), Washington (saw nothing), Maryland (madly ran)

Test Nine Answer 14
peaceful

It is restful or serene. The rest are sluggish or lethargic

Test Nine Answer 15
56: repeat the individual numbers on the top line in the second line, starting at 8. Do the same for lines 3 and 4, starting at 2.

Test Nine Answer 16
VUTS

Reverse the second set of letters in alphabetical sequence. i.e TU - WV (instead of VW)

Test Nine Answer 17
648: x3, x2

Test Nine Answer 18
eastbound

Test Nine Answer 19
9 : 479 + 286 = 765

Test Nine Answer 20
God save the King

Test Nine Answer 21
2200
(330 ÷ 15) x 100 = 2200

Test Nine Answer 22
derange

Test Nine Answer 23
Esteem, respect

Test Nine Answer 24
4½
Add 1¾ at each stage

Test Nine Answer 25
deer

Test Nine Answer 26
22, 78

There are two interwoven sequences. Add 5.5 starting at 0. Subtract 5.5 starting at 100.

Test Nine Answer 27
Luck:
All words can be converted to birds by changing the initial letter: vulture, bustard, finch, raven, gull, crow and duck

Test Nine Answer 28
ostracism, banishment

Test Nine Answer 29
B: Looking across numbers progress +3. Looking down numbers progress +4

Test Nine Answer 30
art: chart, quart and artist, artery

Test Nine Answer 31
water

Test Nine Answer 32
7: 14 x 3 = 42. 42 ÷ 6 = 7

Test Nine Answer 33
mock, real

Test Nine Answer 34
21: looking across and down each line of numbers, the first number in small type is the sum of the first digits of the numbers in bold, and the second number in small type is the sum of the second digits.

Test Nine Answer 35
C

Test Nine Answer 36
rationale

Test Nine Answer 37
perfunctory

Test Nine Answer 38
pitch

Test Nine Answer 39
one man's meat is another man's poison

Test Nine Answer 40
4379

In all the others add the first two digits to obtain the third digit, and the first and third digits to obtain the fourth (and fifth if applicable).

Test Ten | Solutions

Test Ten Answer 1
1 hour 29 minutes
27 + 37 + 15 minutes

Test Ten Answer 2
ua: it does not appear in *the sequence below*.
T (H (E)   S) E Q (U (E) N) C (E   B) (E (L) O) W

Test Ten Answer 3
ARC A MOON = macaroon
The elements are: tungsten (snug tent), magnesium (immune gas), platinum (tulip man), carbon (no crab)

Test Ten Answer 4
Construe

Test Ten Answer 5
Act your age

Test Ten Answer 6
seal: the consonants TRSLDN are being repeated in the same order.

Test Ten Answer 7
track

Test Ten Answer 8
18.5: add 3.7 each time

Test Ten Answer 9
positive, doubtful

Test Ten Answer 10
C: looking across deduct 4, 4, 4, 1, 1. Looking down deduct 1, 1, 1, 4, 4.

Test Ten Answer 11
nip in the bud

Test Ten Answer 12
56 minutes: (80 x 14) ÷ 20

Test Ten Answer 13
commission

Test Ten Answer 14
metre, inch, gram

Test Ten Answer 15
156;   9 + 6 = **15** and 2 + 4 = **6**

Test Ten Answer 16
seminar

Test Ten Answer 17
BARE TOP = PROBATE. The plants are heather, primula, tobacco and thistle.

Test Ten Answer 18
Jackpot

Test Ten Answer 19
smith: all words in column A can be prefixed with black. All words in column B can be prefixed with white.

Test Ten Answer 20
mania: all other words end with two consecutive letters of the alphabet.

Test Ten Answer 21
hang by a thread

Test Ten Answer 22
negate

Test Ten Answer 23
E: the black dot moves 45° clockwise, the white dot moves 90° clockwise and the line moves 45° anti-clockwise.

Test Ten Answer 24
laxness

Test Ten Answer 25
knife and fork

Test Ten Answer 26
the letter S.
In each square start at the middle and work anti-clockwise to spell out short, sharp and shock.

Test Ten Answer 27
168 spots

Since 14 is one third of 42, each fish has the equivalent of 14 spots after two thirds of the male fish have been removed. The answer is, therefore, 12 x 14 = 168.

Test Ten Answer 28
surveillance

Test Ten Answer 29
cog

Test Ten Answer 30
5: 38 - 24 = 14, 36 + 34 = 70, 70 / 14 = 5

Test Ten Answer 31
Hercules: ash, toe, far, arc, you, pal, hoe, was

Test Ten Answer 32
generator

Test Ten Answer 33
seasonal; to produce base/seal, bias/ashy, neon/onus, coal/alas

Test Ten Answer 34
chant: it means sing, and the rest are talk.

Test Ten Answer 35
flatter

Test Ten Answer 36
643: the amount subtracted increases by 17 each time.

Test Ten Answer 37
frigate: the grid contains all names of types of sea going vessels

Test Ten Answer 38
10: each square group of 4 numbers totals 21

Test Ten Answer 39
7: the numbers formed by opposite pairs of digits are in the ration 1 : 3
That is: 75/25, 42/14, 96/32, 81/27, 45/15

Test Ten Answer 40
duplicate, facsimile